THE CELTIC WORLD

An Illustrated History

THE CELTIC WORLD

An Illustrated History

700 B.C. TO THE PRESENT

PATRICK LAVIN

HIPPOCRENE BOOKS INC.
NEW YORK

ISBN 0-7818-0731-X

For information, address:
HIPPOCRENE BOOKS, INC.
171 Madison Avenue
New York, NY 10016

Printed in the United States of America

To Maggie and Abbie

ACKNOWLEDGMENTS

I am grateful to many individuals whose encouragement and help has made this book possible. I am especially grateful to my wife, Joan, for her support and mainstay through all of the ups and downs of research and writing. Her invaluable help and numerous, useful suggestions added much to the enhancement and clarity of the text. I wish to thank Ann Westlake, a skilled professional, whose perceptive editing smoothed out the rough edges.

There were others, of course, who contributed in different ways, and I would like to acknowledge their support: Kara Migliorelli of Hippocrene Books, my agent Elisabet McHugh and my daughter Edie. The many Celtic historians I have consulted will be evident throughout the book and are acknowledged in the bibliography.

CONTENTS

INTRODUCTION

The Celts stand out as one of the most daring of all the ancient European people in the history of pre-Roman Europe. They evolved at a time when written history existed only in the eastern Mediterranean area; consequently, historians have had to rely almost entirely upon archaeological evidence to piece together their obscure origin. The few classical references for the era before 400 B.C. that survive provide little about them apart from a geographical footnote or two.

Celtic culture forged ahead alongside the development of iron technology in Europe, and its growth and achievements have been seen as the marvel of the European Iron Age. Subjugated by the Romans and overshadowed by Roman civilization from the first century B.C., the Celts enjoyed a cultural revival after the collapse of the Roman Empire that was to leave an astonishing legacy to the modern world. From art and music to literature and religion (first pagan and then Christian), their contribution to the maturing of European civilization has been in many ways unique. Celtic traditions have endured, and their legacy includes a host of famous place-names. The great rivers of northern and central Europe: the Rhine, Danube, Neckar, Thames and many others owe their names to remote Celtic antiquity, as do great cities like Paris, Chartres, York and London.[1] Yet, the Celts always were and still are an enigma.

Long before they were conquered by the Anglo-Saxons and then by the Normans, Celtic society prevailed in most of Great Britain and Ireland. From the Orkney Islands to the

Cornwall peninsula and from Galway Bay to the North Sea, the language, political divisions, institutions, laws and way of life were all Celtic. All of these formed a part of the great Celtic peoples who occupied and ruled much of continental Europe before being subjugated by the conquering Roman legions.

Ireland, never invaded by Rome, has preserved a unique storehouse of uninterrupted Celtic history and legend which has kept alive the potency of Celtic culture throughout the centuries. During the Dark Ages when learning, scholarship and culture all but disappeared in Western Europe, Ireland was the site of one of the most incredible literary, artistic and intellectual flourishings western civilization knew; and, if it were not for the holy men and women of Ireland, the great heritage of western civilization might have been lost altogether.

Celtic culture and language have prevailed despite many setbacks throughout history. Gaelic is still spoken in the *Gaeltacht* along the western seaboard of Ireland. Welsh continues to be widely spoken throughout much of Wales, and the Welsh continue to honor their ancient Celtic bardic tradition each year at the National Eisteddfod. On the Isle of Man, Manx is still spoken by many of the islanders. Breton, the most widely spoken Celtic language in Europe, is the language of the people of Brittany. The Scottish Highlanders are proud of their Celtic language (akin to Irish Gaelic) and heritage, as are their descendants who colonized the province of Nova Scotia in Canada. Cornish, although extinct since 1777 when the last native speaker died, is making a comeback.

---

[1]Lloyd Laing, (1979)

MAPS

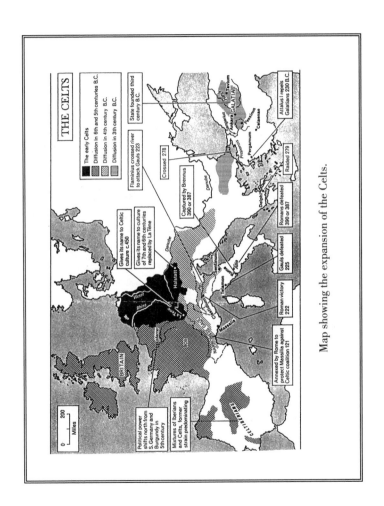

Map showing the expansion of the Celts.

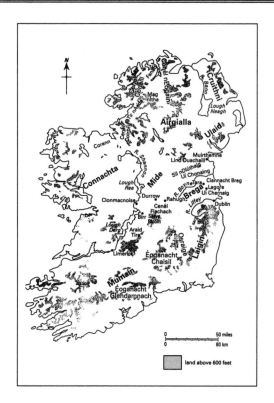

Map of Ireland *c.* 750 A.D. showing major tribal groups.

Ireland's Major Dynasties in the 9ᵀᴴ Century.

CHAPTER I

THE CRADLE OF CELTIC CIVILIZATION

We still know little about how the Celts arose. It is certain only that they were not immigrants, but came from a process of biological and cultural fusion that cannot as yet be analyzed.

— Rudolf Poritnor
Before the Romans Came

The Celtic people arrived on the European stage in prehistoric times as a "fierce naked warrior class that collected enemy heads as war trophies," and evolved into a singular culture that flourished during the European Iron Age. They laid the foundation of western European civilization; before the rise of the Roman Empire, their influence was felt across Europe from Asia Minor to the Atlantic seaboard. A remarkable people endowed with artistic talent and technological skills, the Celts were among the finest metal craftsmen of the ancient world. Their style of art was considered to be one of the great achievements of early Europe. It was the Celts who invented chain armor, though they often preferred to fight naked. They were the first to shoe horses and to shape handsaws, chisels and other tools. Moreover, they invented seamless iron rims for their chariot wheels, the iron plow share, and for the rotary flour mill. In fact, it would not be an overstatement to say that it was the Celts who created Europe's first major industrial revolution.

1

Portion of the circle, Stonehenge.

HISTORICAL SOURCES

What we know of the Celts comes from the Romans, their conquerors, and from the weapons and ornaments they buried with their dead. The oldest surviving classical references to the Celts are very brief and purely casual. Herodotus, writing in the mid-fifth century B.C., mentions them in reference to the source of the Danube which he mistakenly took to be near Pyrene—later believed to have been the Greek trading station Pyrenees on the northeast Spanish coast. Herodotus also mentions Celtic tribes living beyond the Pillars of Hercules (Strait of Gibraltar), which would suggest that they were established on the west coast of the Iberian peninsula as well.

Hecataeus, a historian (c. 540–475 B.C.) whose work is only known from later references, described the Greek trading colony of Massilia (Marseilles) as having been founded in the land of the Ligurians near the land of the Celts. In another reference he recounted a Celtic colony called Nyrax, later believed to have been Noreia in the ancient region of Norcium (closely akin to the present province of Styria in Austria). Ephorus, writing in the fourth century B.C., counted the Celts as one of four "great barbarian" peoples of the known world, the other three being the Sythians, Persians and Libians. In the following century, the geographer Eratosthenes named the Celts as the predominant tribes in western and central Europe.

In eastern Europe the Celts first show up in classical writings in 369–368 B.C., when bands of them were serving as mercenaries for the Peloponnese. This suggests that they had migrated into the Balkans well before this date.[1]

3

WHO ARE THE CELTS?

The Celts are a branch of the Indo-European family from which most of the present-day European, Middle Eastern and Indian races are descended. Their forebears are thought to have lived in the region of the Volga steppes in what is now western Russia. Originally hunters, they evolved into semi-nomadic herders and are given credit for domesticating the horse. By 3000 B.C., they began drifting away from the steppes into the lush valleys of central Europe where a contingent settled in the Alpine region of Austria. There, among indigenous tribes who occupied much of what is now Hungary and western Romania along the middle Danube, they established a tripartite caste system of aristocratic warrior-lord, farmer and serf that matured into a Bronze Age people known as the Urnfielders (so named by archaeologists because they buried the cremated remains of their dead in urns in flat cemeteries). By the twelfth century B.C., urned cremation had spread throughout the heart of Europe to present-day Italy, eastern France, Switzerland, Germany and southern Poland.[2]

It is now generally acknowledged that the Urnfielders were the immediate ancestors to the Celts. Both groups had similar behavioral patterns, and philologists suggest that the Urnfielders may have spoken an early form of Celtic. Thus, it is commonly accepted that in this region and among these folks, to whose genes were added those of successive peoples, there emerged sometime between 1200 and 700 B.C. the coherent society we collectively know as the Celts. Contemporaries marveled at their military prowess and fearless temperament; the Romans dreaded them. But, as German

4

historian Mommsen remarked, "They shook all empires but founded none."

The Celts, in the true sense of the word, were not a pureblood race (don't tell that to any of their descendants!), but were in fact a mixture of many peoples brought together by similarity of religion, custom and language. They have evolved over time into a powerful and enduring culture that has influenced the composition of contemporary nation communities all the way from western Europe to the Americas and the South Pacific.

EMERGENCE OF THE HALLSTATT CULTURE

The earliest definitive archaeological evidence distinguishing the Celtic people as a distinct culture dates from the seventh century B.C. in what is called the Hallstatt period, named after a village in the Salzkammergut in Austria near where prehistoric salt and iron mines were discovered. The foremost technological characteristic that separated the Hallstatt tribes from their Urnfield predecessors was the substitution of iron for bronze in weapons and tools. The use of iron is believed to have originated with the Scythians who, incidentally, are considered by some historians as the progenitors of the Celtic people. This new technology may have reached the early Celtic society by way of the Etruscans, located across the Alps in northern Italy. With the new metal tools, crops were planted and harvested more efficiently, farming became more productive, and the population expanded. Another characteristic which distinguished the Hallstatt culture from that of the Urnfielders was the manner in which burials were carried out. Entombment had replaced cremation as the means of disposing of the dead. Numerous archaeological finds of Late Bronze Age "barrow graves" from northeast France to Bohemia depict members of an aristocratic class entombed in spacious chamber graves, surrounded by an array of personal belongings: a four-wheeled wagon, weapons, bronze horse harness trappings, pottery and the essentials for an after-life feast. The largest barrow grave of this period (analysis dates the walls of the chamber to 550 B.C.) is the Magdalenenberg site in Germany's Black Forest district, measuring 325 feet in diameter.

By the sixth century these early Celts were forming rich settlements run by unified dynasties over a broad range of central and western Europe. The birth of this society was conspicuous by the establishment of citadels, or fortresses, in high places overlooking vast tracts of land. Archaeological finds have yielded much information showing these early Celts as having a dynamic culture with a clan-based society ruled by powerful princes. The one essential element linking the Hallstatt tribes was a common language. They all spoke dialects of a branch of Indo-European now known as Celtic. In their early development, they lived alongside Germanic tribes in what is now southern Germany and Austria, but their social and political forms were quite distinct from that of their neighbors.

By the sixth century B.C. the Hallstatt Celtic society had expanded from western Czechoslovakia (Bohemia) and upper Austria (Norcium), to the upper Rhine, southwest Germany, Helvetia and Burgundy.

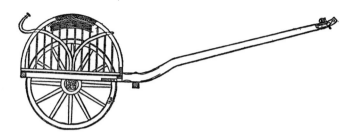

Reconstruction of an early Celtic chariot.

THE LA TENE ERA

There emerged around 500 B.C. a new Celtic cultural phase known in archaeological parlance as the La Tene period. Archaeological evidence from burial grounds and settlement sites suggests that the transition from Hallstatt to La Tene emanated from a growing conflict among members of the ruling class and the low living standards of the masses, whose numbers were rapidly increasing.

What especially distinguished La Tene from the Hallstatt period was the use of elaborate and beautiful decoration on artifacts, as well as a change in burial rite. Instead of interning their dead elite on a four-wheeled wagon as was the practice of the Hallstatt people, they buried them on a more elegant two-wheel chariot, accompanied as before by weapons and the essentials of an after-life feast. Chariots found in fifth century B.C. graves reveal the product of skilled craftsmen, superior in many ways to Greek and Roman craftsmen at the time.

Beaked flagon, whole and two details; bronze and coral.

One of the most extraordinary Celtic tombs discovered in France in the twentieth century belonged to a woman about thirty-five years of age who died around 480 B.C. This woman, known as the princess of Vix, most likely was a powerful personage in her day, evident from the objects placed in her grave. Near Mont Lassois in eastern France, her remains were found lying on a small chariot whose wheels had been removed. Several ornaments and utensils were found alongside the chariot: an enormous bronze krater with lid believed to have been from southern Italy, a silver cup with a gilded ornamented boss protected by a fiber covering, two Greek cups and a bronze Etruscan wine flagon. Placed along a wall of the chamber were Etruscan bowls said to resemble ones depicted in frescoes at Tarquinia in central Italy. On the ground were blue and red pigments thought to be from cloths or decorative paintings. The princess was adorned with a collar made of large stone and amber beads, bronze ankle rings, lignite (coal) bracelets, and fibulae with coral studs, and on her neck was a huge torque, a masterpiece in pure gold believed to have been crafted by a Celtic goldsmith familiar with Mediterranean techniques. Excavations in the nineteenth century of Late Iron Age Celtic cemeteries at Champagne in northeastern France revealed numerous graves in which men (obviously the most important ones) were buried on their chariots wearing bronze helmets, accompanied by their armaments and horse's gear.

The La Tene period also marks the era when the Celts first extended their dominance across the last stages of western European pre-history and into the first pages of history. They initially extended their influence over the area formerly occupied by their Hallstatt predecessors. Their fierce armies of shaggy-haired, mustachioed half-naked warriors touched civilization itself as they expanded their quest for territorial advantage. Ferocious in battle, they horrified the enemy by cutting off the heads of their victims and attaching them to the necks of their horses. They would later be embalmed in cedar oil and displayed as trophies on the walls of their houses.

La Tene Celtic warriors were accustomed to great feasting, drinking and listening to bards boastfully sing of the glories and deeds of their dead heroes and themselves after the fight. Even in their merriment they were prone to fight, sometimes with fatal results. Death, we are told, meant little to them. They believed their soul would survive in another body, or conceivably in the recreation of the present one. Historian Diodorus Siculus wrote of them in the first century B.C.: "They are very tall in stature, with rippling muscles under clear white skin. Their hair is blond, but not naturally so: they bleach it, to this day, artificially, washing it in lime and combing it back from their foreheads. They look like wood-demons, their thick and shaggy hair like a horse's mane. Some of them are clean-shaven, but others—particularly those of high rank—shave their cheeks but leave a mustache that covers the whole mouth . . . They wear brightly colored and embroidered shirts, with trousers called *bracae* and cloaks fastened at the shoulder with a brooch, heavy in winter, light in summer. These cloaks are striped or checkered in design, with the separate checks close together and in various colors."

The Romans called them *Galli* and regarded them as "barbarians" who could neither speak a civilized language nor write any language at all. To the Greeks, they were the *Keltoi* or *Galatai*. Yet their mastery in technology was equal, and in some respects superior, to that of their civilized Greek and Roman counterparts. From the abundance of archaeological evidence unearthed in recent times in the form of exquisite jewelry and metal work, we now know that during the La Tene era Celtic civilization evolved and flourished throughout Europe for several hundred years before the rise of the Roman Empire.

THE CELTIC LANGUAGE

The Celts spoke a language belonging to the great Indo-European family of languages which included Teutonic, Balto-Slavonic and the classical languages of Greek and Latin. In the philological vernacular it is known as Celtic, and it is recognizably akin to the surviving Celtic dialects of the present time. Much of what is known about the Celtic language has come to us through the Classics in the names of chieftains and tribes, and in particular words and terms recorded as belonging to the Celtic people. There are other sources as well, including inscriptions incorporating Celtic words and names (but mainly written in Latin and more rarely in Greek) on altars and other monuments in the Celtic regions of the former Roman Empire, even spanning from Britain to Asia Minor. Celtic place names have survived widely in France, Spain and northern Italy, and to a lesser degree eastwards to Belgrade. In northwest Germany they are common to the Rhine. The distributional evidence of Celtic place names in western and central Europe conforms closely with the regions in which the Celts are known to have been the strongest, and in which their influence lasted the longest.

---

[1] T.G.E. Powell, *The Celts* (1960)

[2] Gerhard Herm, *The Celts* (1977)

CHAPTER 2

CELTIC EXPANSION

Celtic tribes of the Hallstatt culture were settled chiefly in southern Germany and in part of Bohemia, which has preserved in its name that of the original Celtic inhabitants, the *Boii*. In the late Hallstatt era they occupied much of central Europe including Czechoslovakia and parts of Gaul. However, the principal aspect of Celtic expansion began *c.* 500 B.C., and over the next several centuries Celtic tribes went on to conquer and settle most of central and much of southern Europe. Archaeological evidence suggests that one of the primary reasons for this expansionism was the emergence of a new order of warrior aristocracies that began to replace the late Hallstatt culture chieftain class; consequently, a new culture was forged, whose members were predatory and expansionist. This event may be looked upon as the time when the Celtic people moved out of the obscurity of barbarian Europe and into the civilized world of the Mediterranean, passing from prehistory to history.

The first victims of the Celtic expansion were the northern Etruscans, a talented society that had then reached the peak of its five centuries of history. Polybuis, an Arcadian Greek, tells how the Celts "without warning . . . launched a large force against the Etruscans, drove them from their lands around the Po and settled the plains themselves. . . ." The *Insubres* tribes, the first arrivals, eventually established a center at *Mediolanum* (presently Milan). They were followed by at least four other tribes that settled in Lombardy. Later, the *Boii* and *Lingones* settled in Emilia, and the *Senones* settled along the Adriatic coast in Umbria.

FIRST ROMAN ENCOUNTER

South of the Etruscan zone of influence, the community that would evolve into the Roman Empire was taking the first uncertain steps towards statehood. Celtic[1] aggressors headed south, and in 387 B.C. attacked Rome and sacked the city. The besieged Romans had no choice but to enter negotiations, and the Celt's ransom settlement inflicted a lasting wound on Roman pride. Rome remained a prime target for Celtic attacks until the Battle of Telamon in 225 B.C., when the Romans won a decisive victory over a vast Celtic army. But it was not until 192 B.C. that Celtic domination of the northern Italian peninsula came to an end after the Romans defeated the *Boii* tribes on a battlefield near present-day Bologna.

GALATIA

To the east, Celtic tribes moved against the Carpathians, and soon after devastated Macedonia, which only half a century earlier had been the hub of the greatest empire the ancient world had previously known. They fought the Athenians and pillaged Delphi, the sacred shrine of Apollo and the Pythoness. Celtic mercenaries were frequently found in Hellenistic armies in the third century. King Alexander the Great, campaigning in Bulgaria in 335 B.C., received delegations from the peoples living along the lower Danube including an emissary from the Celts. The most curious adventure by Celtic tribes was that undertaken into Asia Minor. They were invited there originally by an aristocratic knight from Bythina on the Bosphorus who persuaded them to fight for him against the Seleucid Aniochus, who then claimed sovereignty over all Asia Minor and dominions beyond. By 270 B.C. they had permanently settled an area of northern Phrygia, thereafter named Galatia. Although they were cut off from their European roots, these Galatians (as they came to be known) managed to retain their Celtic customs and language into early Christian times. They are mentioned in the New Testament in St. Paul's Epistle to the Galatians where he admonishes them not only against idolatry, sorcery and jealousy, but just as strongly against hatred, murder, drunkenness, and the like.

IBERIAN PENINSULA

The Iberian Peninsula had been widely Celticized from early in the La Tene period, probably before 450 B.C. Celtic tribes first penetrated Gaul, then crossed over the Pyrenees where they intermarried with the indigenous population and became known as Celti-Iberians. The historian Diodorus, describing the Celti-Iberians, recounts their many features, similar to those of the inhabitants of northern Italy and Gaul: ". . . Cruel and [at the same time] hospitable, brilliant iron-smiths and formidable warriors. They march into battle singing, and sang as they attacked. They were as proficient on horseback as on foot; they had weaponry and clothing much like the Gauls, wearing trousers, woolen cloaks and plumed helmets. They specialized in surprise attacks for plunder; a lightening advance out of the hills was followed by equally rapid withdrawal into the undergrowth or the rocks, as the Romans would repeatedly learn to their cost. . . ." Communities of Celts still survive in modern Spain in the northern provinces of Galicia, Asturias and Cantabria.

GAUL

The Celts occupied a large part of present-day France and Belgium (Gaul) from an early period. The Celts, according to classical historians, did not enter Gaul as a single nation. They appear to have arrived as military units, each occupying a more or less defined river valley; and, in the course of conquest and settlement, these separate elements formed political and military unions with the indigenous inhabitants of the area. As early as 400 B.C. they had pushed south to the ancient territory of the *Ligurians* and formed the Celto-Ligurian League under a single chief who led them against the wealthy Greek trading colony at Massilia (Marseilles). To the north, Belgae tribes crossed the Rhine into Gaul in the fourth and third centuries B.C., pushed forward by pressure from the German tribes. According to Caesar, they claimed to be of pure Teutonic origin, but they spoke a Celtic language and their leaders bore Celtic names, so it is possible that they were of Celtic origin with a later Teutonic intermixture. By Caesar's time the Celts clearly dominated most of Gaul (present-day France, Belgium and Switzerland).[2]

BRITAIN AND IRELAND

Celtic influence in Britain first came about by trade and the occasional isolated settlement of Hallstatt immigrants who, for the most part, assimilated into the island's indigenous Bronze Age population. In Britain, as in Ireland, the La Tene culture became well established early on, with the arrival of Gaulish and Belgae tribes from that part of Gaul which lies to the south of present-day Belgium. In the first century B.C. there were further invasions by Belgae tribes, whose influence on Britain led to a greater flowering of Celtic culture, particularly in the south. They are credited with establishing trade links with Rome—a move some historians believe set the stage for the Roman conquest of Britain.

THE PAN-CELTIC WORLD

The third century marked the peak of Celtic expansion at which time Celtic people occupied a vast area stretching from Ireland in the west to the Black Sea in the east. They rubbed shoulders with the Hellenistic world in the East, exposing their culture to more affluence than that of their kinfolk in the west. But, as Gerhard Herm suggests, the Celts' greatest error was that they relied too much upon "natural superiority," and never undertook the hard work of exploiting and organizing their resources.[3] Creating the La Tene culture seemed easy to them, but they failed when it came to empire building.

---

[1] Commonly referred to as Gauls, as Roman historians thought they had come from the northwest.

[2] Nora Chadwick, *The Celts* (1997)

[3] Gerhard Herm, *The Celts* (1977)

CHAPTER 3

COLLAPSE OF THE CELTIC WORLD

> The whole [Celtic] race . . . is madly fond of war, high
> spirited and quick to battle, but otherwise straightfor-
> ward and not of evil character. And so when they are
> stirred up they assemble in their bands for battle,
> quite openly and without forethought, so that they are
> easily handled by those who desire to outwit them.
>
> —Strabo

The Celts renewed their hostilities against Rome in 285
B.C., but this time they suffered a major setback when
the Romans assembled a powerful army against them. The
Celtic world began to disintegrate when their domination in
the eastern Mediterranean came to an end after encountering
defeats in Macedonia, and at Pergamon in Turkey in 244 B.C.
Celtic armies suffered further defeats, climaxing at the Battle
of Telamon in 225 B.C., when all Celtic tribes south of the
River Po were brought under Roman influence.

OFFENSIVE FROM GERMANIC TRIBES

In the second century Celts and Romans alike felt the
scourge of another group—Germanic *Cimbri* and Teuton
tribes from the shores of the North Sea and Jutland—who
besieged Celtic and Roman territories from 113 to 101 B.C.
The *Cimbri* made their first appearance around 113 B.C.

when a disastrous tidal wave forced them to leave their homeland in the Jutland peninsula and move southwards; their attempts to resettle in Celtic territory met with fierce opposition from the *Boii* and other Celtic tribes. In 109 B.C. the *Cimbri* joined forces with the Teutons and the *Helvetii* and marched to a position near the Rhone where they met and routed a Roman army commanded by the consul Silenus.

Four years later the *Cimbri*, Teutons and *Helvetii* joined forces again, and with a crack force of *Ambrones* marched down the Rhone. At Orange they met and defeated a Roman army led by Servilius Cepio and Mallius Maximus. The *Cimbri* next pushed over the Pyrenees into Spain while the Teutons continued southwards across Gaul destroying everything that stood in their way. Their only effectual opposition came from the Belgae, but even they could not prevent the invaders from establishing a colony along the banks of the river Sambre near Namur. It was this colony of Teutons (the *Atuatuci* tribe) that was so harassing to Caesar during his conquest of Gaul. The *Helvetii* journeyed back up the Rhone to settle beyond Lake Geneva only to be driven from the region later by the *Surevi* under Ariovistus.

The *Cimbri* crossed back over the Pyrenees in 103 B.C. and joined the Teutons in a carefully planned advance on Italy. The Romans, all too mindful of the danger of a Cimbrian-Teuton coalition, recalled Marius[1] from Africa to take them on. Instead of following France's south coast which they knew would be well-defended by the Romans, the invaders decided to cross over the Alps and surprise their foe from the rear. Marius, a skilled military leader, took on the Teutons first; his successful encounter against them in a battle near Pourrieres resulted in large-scale slaughter, not only among the two armies, but also among the Teuton women and children who followed their men everywhere. The battle at Pourrieres was long remembered by the Romans as a turning point in their conquest of Gaul. Meanwhile, the *Cimbri* continued their march through the northern Alps. Having routed the consul Catulus at Adige, the road to Rome lay open before them. Instead of making straight for a defenseless Rome, they dispersed to look for plunder and to wait for their allied Teuton forces (unaware they had been decimated by Marius and his Roman legions). Marius showed up to the surprise of the *Cimbri*, who then resorted to threatening the Romans with dreadful consequences when they arrived in Italy. "They are here," shouted the consul as he marched out Teutoboduus and the Teuton chiefs in chains. When the *Cimbri* realized what had happened, they asked Marius to select a site for a final encounter. On July 3, 101 B.C., both sides met near Verceil and the battle proved to be just as terrible a massacre as Pourrieres. The Romans were once again victorious, and the Cimbrian threat was removed once and for all.

Posidonius, regarded as an authority on the subject, maintains that the *Cimbri* as well as the Teutons were Celtic; Strabo on the other hand claimed they were Germanic tribes.[2] The evidence suggests, however, that they were more Celtic than Germanic: they spoke a Celtic language, associated themselves with Celtic tribes (the *Helvetii*, for example), all had Celtic names, and *Cimbrian* prophetesses were akin to the Celtic priestesses.[3] All this collaborates the theory held by many historians that the Celtic world was no more than a melange of different tribes and ethnic groups under a Celtic elite in which the indigenous peoples of the lands they conquered were first enslaved and then fused by a common Celtic language, culture and religion.

THE ROMAN OFFENSIVE

During the first half of the last century B.C., the Romans began their dogged intrusion onto Gaulish territories under an ambitious and brilliant military leader by the name of Julius Caesar, who now ranks alongside Hannibal and Alexander as one of the most remarkable generals of ancient times. Caesar set his sights on conquering all of Gaul (the heartland of Celtic Europe), but had to invent some convincing pretense for his campaign to the Senate. Rome had already occupied northern Italy to maintain peace in the Po valley area between the warring Celtic tribes that had settled there. Rome had sent its legions into Spain to protect its interests from Hannibal's conquering forces, and had annexed a broad strip of land along the Mediterranean coast of France in 125 B.C., turning it into the Roman province of Gallia Narbonensis—a link between Italy and Spain. Up to this point in history Gallic society had not been a threat to Rome's interests, and Caesar knew that any attempts at annexation would meet with fierce resistance from the Gauls. Gaul, however, was a hegemony of self-dependent tribal communities constantly engaged in armed conflict with each other, or with their Germanic neighbors to the north. Caesar was quite sure that sooner or later there would be opportunities to exploit the situation.

Caesar's first entanglement came in 58 B.C. when he led an army north over the Alps against the *Helvetii* and their allied tribes who were attempting to emigrate en masse from their Swiss homeland to southern Gaul (due to a mounting threat from invading Germanic tribes). Caesar blocked their move by destroying a bridge over the Rhone near Genava (Geneva). When they tried to negotiate with him, he turned his legions upon them, massacring more than 6,000 and forcing the remainder back to their homeland. Savoring victory, Caesar returned to northern Italy to attend to urgent administrative affairs and left his legions in charge of his newly acquired territory. Soon after, Caesar began receiving intelligence reports that the *Belgic* tribes had formed a confederation and were readying for war against the Romans. The powerful *Bellovaci* tribe from the Oise region were in charge of the campaign, and among the others participating were the *Suessiones*, the *Nervii*, the *Atrebates*, the *Ambiani*, the *Morini,* the *Menapii*, the *Calati,* the *Veliocasses*, the *Viromandui* and the Teutonic *Atuatuci*. The *Remi* refused to join and made an alliance with Caesar. Alarmed by the reports, Caesar raised two new legions and intensified his intelligence-gathering network along the Belgae frontier. Disturbed by the reports, he moved quickly and victoriously to thwart the Belgae siege of a fortress near Bibrax. Caesar's decisive battle against the Belgae, however, was on the banks of the Aisne where Roman legions out-maneuvered and pushed back the enemy. Determined to exploit this victory, Caesar entered the land of the *Suessiones*, besieged their capital, *Noviodunum*, and forced them to surrender. He next went after the *Bellovaci* and they also capitulated. Meanwhile, the *Nervii*, who had a reputation for tenacity, joined forces with the *Atrebates* and the *Viromandui* and took on the Romans at Sambre in a brutal encounter. The Roman side, stunned by a ferocious onslaught which inflicted severe casualties, was finally saved from massacre by the skillful maneuvering of their military leaders and by the arrival of reinforcements.

Caesar sent his legions into Armorica (present-day Britanny) in 56 B.C. against the *Veneti*, the greatest of the four Armorican peoples. The *Veneti*, relying on their powerful fleet and cross channel support, were defeated by an armada of Roman ships under Caesar's lieutenant, Publius Crassus, at the battle in Morbihan Bay. They had staked and lost everything and were a conquered country.

It was at Alesia that the *Carnutes* and their allies, under the leadership of Vercingetorix, an Arvernian prince, put up a last desperate stand against Caesar's legions. Vercingetorix's grand plan to reclaim much of Gaul from Caesar's grasp was foiled by superior Roman strategy, and he was eventually forced to surrender due to dwindling food supplies. Legend has it that he dressed in his finest armor, mounted his best horse and rode into the Roman camp where he prostrated himself before Caesar.

This victory brought Caesar triumph over Gaul and brought about the collapse of a great nation—but not of a great people. In exchange for individuality and pride, the Gauls acquired the amenities of a higher civilization and the confidence that Roman law would bring an end to centuries of restless warfare and inter-tribal feuding. Over the next few years Caesar had just a few local revolts to contend with. Celtic Gaul was divided into four Roman provinces—*Narbonensis*, *Aquitania*, *Lugdunensis* and *Belgica*—and tribal leaders had to submit to Rome's laws, administration, and agree to an annual tax of four million sesterces (equivalent to coins weighing forty-five tons in silver). Four thousand Gallic volunteers were inducted into the Roman military as an autonomous legion, and some Gallic leaders were even assigned to Caesar's personal staff.

CELTI-IBERIAN RESISTANCE

The Iberian peninsula had been widely Celticized since the early La Tene period when tribes from the north crossed the Pyrenees and intermarried with the indigenous population to form the Celti-Iberians. Later, the *Galicians* emerged in the extreme northwest, the *Lusitanians* in modern Portugal, along with lesser tribes such as the *Vaccaei*. The Iberian Peninsula (at least its former Celtic parts) had fallen to Rome in the Second Punic War when Publius Cornelius Scipio conquered the western Phoenicians. In doing so, he succeeded in presenting himself to the native Celti-Iberians as their liberator from foreign domination.

The goodwill did not last, and the inhabitants launched a guerrilla war in which the legionaries once more faced the onslaught of ferocious attacks. It was on the Iberian Peninsula that the Celtic (*Arevacian*) tribes gained such a fearful reputation that Roman soldiers refused to fight them. To confront the problem, Rome sent its best general, Scipio Aemilianus, with no less than sixty thousand legionaries to combat the four-thousand-man garrison of *Numantia*. Believing that his army was not strong enough to attempt an attack, Aemilianus proceeded instead with a blockade. For sixteen months the gallant Celts held out, then burned their dwellings and killed themselves rather than surrender to the Romans.

It took Rome two hundred years to completely subdue the Celtic tribes of the Iberian Peninsula. It was the campaign of Emperor Augustus in the Cantabrian Wars of 29–19 B.C. that finally brought about an end to the hostilities from the Cantabrians, Austurians and Galicians.

THE BRITISH CAMPAIGN

The Romans went on to defeat the Celts in Britain in 47 A.D., establishing a Roman province on the island. A struggle for dominance among the British Celts led to Verica, leader of the *Atrebates*, seeking help from Rome. It came when 20,000 legionaries, led by Emperor Claudius, crossed the Channel and established a bridgehead. This was the final step in submerging the Celts into Roman culture. With the exception of a few pockets, Celtic culture on the European mainland ceased to exist. Only beyond the western frontier of the Empire, especially in Wales, Scotland and Ireland, did Celtic culture escape Roman influence. Ireland, in particular, remained outside the realm of Roman control, and Celtic culture endured and flourished there right up until the tenth century. Many believe that Irish Celtic culture continued to have much in common with the Gaulish and Belgae Celts before the Romans subdued them in 58 B.C.

History has been kind to Caesar and his Roman legionaries, for they were the victors in subjugating the "barbarian" Celts. History has been less kind to the Celts, chiefly because it was conveyed by the Roman pen. The roots of the Celts' downfall, however, were already deeply imbedded within the Celtic pathos itself. Individualistic and proud, they were unwilling to accept the concept of peaceful partnership essential to a well-organized central government. Their political institutions functioned in small groups centered around the family. Political coherence on a societal scale escaped them; unlike the Romans, the Celts were not empire builders.

CELTIC HERITAGE LIVES ON

Although the power and political importance of the Celts had declined throughout the Continent, by the beginning of the Christian era their contribution to civilization and art remained of great significance for the evolution of European culture. There is barely a nation in Europe which has not drawn directly or indirectly on the treasure of this Celtic heritage. The mainspring of Celtic traditions and the Celtic heritage, of course, continued in Britain and Ireland, where Celtic culture developed undisturbed after Gaul was subordinated into the Roman Empire. In Ireland, Wales and western Scotland, where neither the Romans nor the Anglo-Saxons secured a permanent foothold, Celtic culture was preserved. From there, the ancient Celtic traditions in the form of literature and other art forms came to a new flowering in the early centuries of the Middle Ages—and this culture reached back to inspire England and the countries of Europe during the Dark Ages.

---

[1] Third founder of Rome after Romulus and Furius Camillus, and an uncle to Caesar

[2] Gerhard Herm, *The Celts* (1977)

[3] Jean Markale, *The Celts* (1993)

CHAPTER 4

CELTIC BRITAIN

The first account from historical sources mentioning Celts in Britain was from Julius Caesar who reported that there were Belgae settlements in southeastern Britain; among them were the *Suessiones* who also ruled a great area north of the *Marnex* (Marne) River in northern Gaul. He added that in the interior of the island lived "original inhabitants, while on the coast lived those peoples who had come from Belgium with bellicose intentions, to plunder, and who had then stayed on to practice agriculture. Almost all of them bear the names of the tribes they came from."[1]

Other accounts from classical literature with references to Britain and Ireland allude to the possibility of earlier Celtic settlements. In the sixth century B.C. before the year 530 there is mention of a voyage undertaken from Massilia down the east Spanish coast through the Pillars of Hercules, and along the Atlantic seaboard to the city of *Taretessos*. On the ship's return someone wrote an account of the voyage describing the Spanish coasts and lands far to the north along the Atlantic seaways of Europe. This document is known as the *Massilliot Periplus*, and it survives in fragments quoted in the poem *Ora Maritima* by Rufus Festus Avienus who lived in the fourth century A.D. In it Britain is described as *insula Albionum*, and there is mention of *gens Hiernorum* (Irish race).

Around 320 B.C. Pytheas, the Greek explorer, made a voyage north along the western coast of Europe, circumnavigated Britain and sketched a description of the island's main features and of its neighbor, Ireland. Using a transliteration of Gallo-Brettonic, he named them the Pretanic Islands and hence the inhabitants as the Priteni.[2] During the Roman period the designation *Brittones* (thought to be a corruption of Priteni) came into use and from it was derived the name Britain. Thereafter, Priteni is used to refer to the tribes the Romans called *Picti* or Picts. It is now commonly acknowledged from archaeological evidence that cultural links along the Atlantic seaboard from Portugal to Britain extend far back in time.

PRIMORDIAL INHABITANTS

The first known invasion of Britain is believed to have occurred eight to ten thousand years ago when Mesolithic people arrived by way of a land connection between the island and the European mainland. They were hunters and food-gatherers, and virtually little is known of them or the period in which they lived. Soon after 4000 B.C., at the dawn of the Neolithic period, the first bands of farmer-immigrants established themselves in the chalk-lands country of southern

30

Britain. Over the next two millennium, came additional settlers of different cultural levels, and probably speaking different languages. The most important legacy they left behind were burial sites: megalithic tombs of the types known as *passage graves* with a passageway from the entrance to a circular burial chamber, and *gallery graves* with a long rectangular chamber. At the end of the fifteenth century B.C., a remarkable early Bronze Age began to flourish alongside the Neolithic communities in the southeastern part of the island. It continued for several hundred years before stagnating and eventually being overtaken by a new technology—the central European Urnfield culture—which spread to the communities of the Atlantic fringe in the Late Bronze Age.[3]

THE ATLANTIC PERIPHERY

The distinguished British archaeologist Barry Cunliffe[4] describes how within the Atlantic periphery, which extended from the Straight of Gibraltar to northern Britain, there evolved a network of four closely linked trading partnerships. The first included southern Ireland, south Wales, southwest Britain and Armorica—all rich in metal resources, principally copper, tin and gold. A second area included the coastal region of Gaul, between the Seine and the Rhine, and the adjacent shores of Britain from Hampshire to East Anglia; here, the most archaeological visible medium of exchange was bronze, either in the form of finished items or scrap. Further to the north, cultural similarities suggest that the communities of north and west Scotland, the Northern and Western Isles, and the northeastern part of Ireland formed another closely related zone. South of Armorica, the archaeological evidence points to two distinctive cultural zones: the northwest corner of Iberia, including Galicia, Austuria and Cantabria, with its highly centralized settlement groups and abundant supplies of gold and tin; and the southwestern zone, stretching from the Tagus to the Lower Guadalquivir, an area rich in copper and silver and recognized for its Late Bronze Age engraved stelae and burnished pottery.

This network of commercial exchanges linking the Atlantic communities and the Urnfield aristocracy in western and central Europe continued to evolve in the ensuing Hallstatt C period. In the subsequent Hallstatt D period a significant change in the pattern and intensity of the trading partnerships occurred, which Cunliffe suggests was the consequence of new trading links arising between the Late Hallstatt elite and the Mediterranean states.

According to Cunliffe, archaeological evidence from Atlantic Europe for the period from 1300 to 200 B.C. identifies three distinct phases. In the first from *c.* 1300 to *c.* 600, described as the most dynamic, the entire Atlantic system north of Galicia was actively engaged in an intricate network of reciprocal exchange with the Urnfield and early Hallstatt societies of west central Europe. Meanwhile, in the south of Iberia, the Phoenicians, and possibly the Greeks, were creating ties with the Mediterranean system. In the second period, from *c.* 600 to *c.* 400, the intensity of the east-west contacts abated noticeably, with Ireland now left outside the system. This lessening is believed to have been caused by a realignment of trading exchanges and routes through Brittany linking the west Hallstatt elites more directly with the metal-rich core of southwestern Britain; at the same time, Mediterranean interests in the Atlantic coast trade increased. In the third and final period, *c.* 400 to *c.* 200, a time of great migratory movements throughout much of central Europe, trading between the communities along the Atlantic seaboard slackened somewhat, but association with Mediterranean entrepreneurs continued.

The profundity and duration of the maritime links which bound the trading partners of the Atlantic Celtic peoples together also provided the bonding that safeguarded and stimulated their common cultural identity. All parts of the Atlantic coastline, from the Shetland Islands to as far south as southwestern Iberia, shared this common culture. Furthermore, it is well established that they all spoke an early form of the Celtic language, the accepted view being that it was Goidelic or Q-Celtic (which continued to be the dominant form in Ireland) as opposed to Brythonic or P-Celtic (which later became the dominant form in Britain and Gaul).

EARLY CELTIC-SPEAKING TRIBES IN BRITAIN

Sometime between 1200 and 1000 B.C., during the Urnfield expansion, an early Celtic-speaking people arrived in Britain, identified as such because their language had not quite developed into a form which would be easily recognizable as Celtic today. Archaeological artifacts and pottery items found in Kent classify them as having come from northeastern Gaul.

By the early part of the eighth century B.C. large-scale migrations took place, and the bulk of archaeological evidence shows that the areas affected were the chalk-lands of present-day Sussex, Dorset and Wiltshire. These newcomers also practiced farming, and some of their farm sites and field systems have survived to the present day. They cremated their dead and placed the ashes in urns for burial, a practice not new to the indigenous population who also cremated their dead. It is thought that these settlers were essentially refugees from the migratory movements, caused by the expansion of the Hallstatt warrior culture which was occurring throughout the northern Alpine region of Europe about that time. Curiously, their colonies in Britain do not appear to have spread greatly beyond their primary chalk-land settlements; archaeological evidence for areas to the north and west equates more to military artifacts belonging to later settlements of the Hallstatt warrior class.

Trading and cultural links were maintained with their Continental kinsfolk and intensified as copper, and later bronze, became available. Contacts intensified further in the Late Bronze Age as all kinds of bronze objects were traded in increasing quantities and over greater distances than before. This evidence comes from the unearthing of artifacts and, in some rare instances, from the recovery of shipwrecks, such as vessels carrying Gaul-made implements which foundered off the Cliffs of Dover and in Saltcomb Bay in Devon roughly at the start of the first millennium.

CELTIC-SPEAKING COLONISTS

It is generally acknowledged that Britain was settled by Celtic-speaking people in three waves. The first wave is believed to have been heralded by trade during the Hallstatt period in the seventh century B.C., bringing with it colonists who established settlements principally on the southern coastal areas of the island. Over time, these settlers became assimilated with the island's indigenous population whose culture and language they replaced with their own.

The second great wave began in the fifth century B.C. at the beginning of the La Tene era, and continued unabated for several centuries as many divergent tribes flocked onto the island from the Continent. The earlier settlers of the second wave, sometimes referred to as "Marnians" (because they were from the Marne River region of northern Gaul), are believed to have formed an overlordship in the areas they occupied. In the north, emigrants from the Champagne area of Gaul established a settlement in east Yorkshire, and archaeological relics recovered from the area show it to be the largest colony of its kind in Britain before the late second century B.C. Pytheas, the fourth century B.C. Greek explorer, recorded that the Celts in Britain were agricultural and pastoral farmers, like their cousins on the Continent. Their main crop was wheat, and he was amazed at the large inland herds of cattle and sheep. In the Cornish peninsula he found the Celtic tribes working iron, tin and bronze, also making fine pottery and spinning and weaving wool and cloth. He found that they preferred to barter goods, refusing to accept coins.[5]

Gold coins, 1ˢᵀ cent. B.C. Above and below, left: *Stater of the Parisii, obverse and reverse.* Right: *Stater of the Bellovaci, obverse and reverse.*

The final phase of colonization in Britain occurred in the century before the Roman conquest. The newcomers were known to Caesar as the Belgae and they came from that part of Gaul which lies just south of present-day Belgium. Their arrival brought changes that on one hand led to a great flowering of Celtic culture in the areas they settled, and on the other hand opened up trade links and contacts with Rome which some historians believe eventually played a role in the Roman conquest of the island. When Caesar led his legions through southern Britain he was surprised to find the countryside heavily populated and the houses closely resembling those in Gaul. Timber was the main building material, although drystone walling was not unusual. He discovered that the inhabitants were experts in working bronze, tin and iron and were accomplished in decorating pottery and drawing curved designs. When fighting, they wore metal helmets beautifully ornamented and inlaid, and some communities in the south of Britain had their own coinage. Brythonic, or P-Celtic,[6] was the universal language of the inhabitants. Their religion was administered by a priestly caste, the druids, a privileged class who were the protectors of the law and the leaders of public opinion, and to whom the mistletoe was a revered emblem. Their most sacred shrine was on the island of Anglesey (Mona) off the northern coast of Wales.

CAESAR'S INCURSIONS INTO BRITAIN

During the Gallic war, Britons fought with the Gauls against the Romans, and, after the war, continued the trading and cultural links that were long-established between the two regions. Caesar, suspicious that the British Druidic religious leaders were aiding and abetting subversive activities across the Channel, made two armed explorations of southeastern Britain in 55 and 54 B.C. to appraise the situation.

On August 25, 55 B.C., the Roman fleet came ashore under the great white cliffs of south Foreland, atop which were massed thousands of Celtic warriors. On the open beaches at Walmer, in the land of the *Cantii*, the Roman fleet dropped anchor; and, after a brief encounter, the Celtic chieftains agreed on opening peace negotiations with Caesar. The peace negotiations went on for several days, during which time a great storm rolled into the area causing extensive damage to Caesar's warships riding at anchor. The Celts saw this as a sign that the gods were on their side and they called off the negotiations. The situation looked bleak for the Romans now on a hostile shore with no provisions or equipment for a protracted winter campaign. Caesar ordered his men into the countryside to forage for food and supplies, but they were ambushed by a large force of Celtic warriors in war-chariots. Caesar led a battalion into action to relieve the pinned-down party, and it was during this encounter that he observed firsthand how the Celts used their war-chariots in battle: "First of all they drive in all directions and hurl javelins, and so by the mere terror that the teams inspire and by the noise of the wheels, they generally throw the ranks of soldiers into confusion. When they have worked their way in between the troops, they leap down from the chariots and fight on foot. Meanwhile their charioteers retire gradually from the battle, and place the chariots in such a fashion that, if the warriors are hard-pressed by the enemy, they may have a ready means of retreat to their own side. . . ."[7]

Caesar later withdrew to the Continent where he began plans for a future campaign to establish a permanent garrison in Britain. He arrived a second time on September 25, 54 B.C., but events in Gaul and a subsequent uprising against Rome dashed any hopes he had of bringing the island into submission. Caesar departed without establishing a permanent settlement, and the turbulent political situation in the Roman world after his assassination delayed any further plans for conquest for another century.

Caesar's brief campaigns in Britain may not have achieved a great deal from a military point of view, but he did succeed in establishing treaty relations with certain tribes on the east coast north of the Thames; thus, he was securing bonds of clientage that would be later used to Rome's political advantage. There are recorded instances in the early part of the first century B.C. of British rulers who fled to Rome seeking help from the emperor in their inter-tribal disputes. The last recorded instance was that of Verica, king of the *Atrebates*, whose appeal to Rome provided Emperor Claudius with the excuse he needed to mount a British invasion.

ROMAN CONQUEST OF BRITAIN

It had been nearly a century since Caesar's aborted military campaign into Britain when the Emperor Claudius launched a new invasion in 43 A.D. resolved at establishing a solid footing for the colonization Caesar had failed to achieve ninety years earlier. The Romanization of Celtic Britain had thus begun.

The Britain into which Claudius' legions arrived in 43 A.D. was a country of separate tribal kingdoms without much political unity. The Belgic tribes occupied a large part of southeastern Britain and as far west as the Cotswolds. Tribes of the *Cantii*, *Trinovantes* and *Iceni*, already partly Romanized, were ready to enter into treaty relationships with the Romans as client states.[8] Further afield were several stubbornly independent Celtic kingdoms, prominent among them the *Parisi* of east Yorkshire and the *Brigantes* who occupied much of northern England. To the far west were several Welsh tribes, equally as independent: the *Cornovii* who occupied the Welsh Marches, the *Ordovices* of North Wales and the *Silures* of South Wales. Northern Britain (present-day Scotland) did not emerge into recorded history until 80 A.D. when the Romans, under Julius Agricola, pushed northward to subdue the "wild and barbaric" tribes of Caledonia. However, archaeological data reveals that the Celtic tribes of Caledonia were certainly as advanced as their Celtic kinsmen elsewhere.

The first advance of the invading force captured Camulodunum, the capital of the *Catuvellauni* tribes, and from there spread out across the core of the southeast to take jurisdiction of the territories either directly or indirectly under the control of the *Catuvellauni*, as well as those of the *Atrebates* whose king, Verica, had sought assistance from Rome. Next, the Romans successfully overpowered the *Durotriges*, *Dobunni* and *Corieltolavi* (but not without considerable resistance from the *Durotriges*), and laid a military road through all three territories; this road was called the Fosse Way, and it ran from one military base at Exeter on the Channel coast to another at Lincoln on the east coast. The southeastern area of the island was now under Roman administration, but for two client kingdoms which Claudius had created within it: the *Iceni* of Norfolk were left under the command of Prasutagus, while the *Atrebates* were put under the control of a leader named Cogidubnus.

It was not all plain sailing for the Romans. As they pushed ahead, they encountered strong opposition from a coalition of Celtic forces organized by Togodubnus and Caratacus, two sons of Cunobelin, king of the *Catuvellauni* who had died a year or so before. Togodubnus was killed in action, and Caratacus fled beyond the hinterland into the Welsh mountains where he kept up resistance to Rome for a number of years.

Rome next negotiated a pact with the *Brigantes*, a coalition of clans occupying most of northern England under the leadership of a Queen Cartimandua. In 51 A.D., Cartimandua kidnapped and handed over Caratacus to the Romans, arousing the fury of anti-Roman dissidents in the kingdom led by her estranged husband Venutius. In the ensuing confrontation, Queen Cartimandua received backing from the Romans to buttress her authority over the dissidents. For the next ten years she succeeded in retaining her position as queen, but then lost it when Venutius gained control after orchestrating a revolt among anti-Roman tribes against her. While these events took place, Roman legions had taken control of the English midlands, the southwestern peninsula and much of Wales with the only significant opposition coming from two major Welsh tribes, the *Silures* in the south and the *Ordovices* in the north. The fighting was fierce, but the superior skills and discipline of the Roman legions ultimately prevailed.

In other areas the Romans achieved limited success as resistance to their occupation mounted. The Romans, suspecting that Druidism was behind much of the resistance, attacked the island of Mona (Anglesey), destroyed the shrine of Druidism and slaughtered most of the druids operating there. Reports show that the Romans encountered no difficulty in occupying the unprotected island, because it never occurred to the Britons that anyone would dare attack this sacred sanctuary. But the sacrilege committed at Mona turned more Britons against the Romans. In 61 A.D. a rebellion by the *Iceni*, led by their queen Boudica (wife of the Roman client king Prasutagus), spread rapidly and ferociously as other disaffected Britons joined in. The Roman colony of Camulodunum, the town of Verulamium and the port of London were destroyed and many of their inhabitants killed. The Romans eventually put down the revolt in a battle where supposedly 80,000 Britons were killed. Boudica ended her life with poison.

Meanwhile the situation in the north of Britain had deteriorated, and Cartimandua had to be rescued. Rome appointed Julius Agricola governor of Britain in 78 A.D. He served for eight years during which time he steadfastly pushed the area of Roman domination northwards to the Briton-Pict border at the Firth of Tay. He led seven campaigns to complete the subjugation of the Caledonian tribes, fighting the last successful battle against the army of Calgacus at Mons Graupius in the far north on the south side of the Moray Firth. Tacitus, his son-in-law, tells how this was the last occasion when a Celtic army used chariots against a Roman force. Mons Graupius marks the culmination of Rome's military victories against the Britons; and, submission of the

Orkney Islands tribes brought Agricola's victorious campaign to an end. However, the Roman hold on northern and western Caledonia was fragile at best, and the Romans ended up withdrawing to what is known as the Tyne-Solway line. Later, emperors Hadrian and Antoninus Pius each had a wall built to prevent incursions by the Picts and by those Britons who had fled into Caledonia. Hadrian's Wall stretched from the Tyne to the Clyde, and Antoninus Pius' Wall along the Firth of Forth.

By this time, the greater part of Britain was under Roman domination. Only Caledonia and the Welsh area of Powys, then occupied by *Ordovices* and Irish tribes, still remained independent. Unlike with Gaul, the occupying forces were content to administer the country militarily, at least until the time of Diocletian. In Gaul, Roman civil administration overlapped the existing framework of *civitates*, while in Britain only military commanders kept a watch over the natives and colonies of veterans. That is why Gallic tribal names survived in the large towns (for example: the *Parisii* in Paris and the *Redones* in Rennes), while British tribal names disappeared.

Over the next several centuries of Roman occupation, the island continued to be governed by military officials who were effectual rulers quite capable, on occasion, of acting in their own interests rather than strictly in Roman interests. In 387 Maximus (the emperor who became more British than the Britons) proclaimed himself emperor and set out from Britain to reconquer rebellious Rome with an army largely composed of Britons. He was beaten by Theodosius as soon as he reached the Continent. Later, Constantine III usurped the title of emperor and crossed over to Gaul where he was confronted by Stilichon.

Under Roman domination few of the average Britons became Romanized; only their leaders adapted Roman customs and chose to live in Roman-style villas. The old socioeconomic divisions at the time of the conquest remained unchanged throughout the Roman interlude. In the commercially-advanced southeast, (south and east of the Fosse Way), native customs were easily adapted to Roman administrative requirements and the economy grew and prospered. In Cornwall, Wales and the north, however, traditional patterns of Celtic living remained unchanged. Latin, the language of the rulers, was scarcely ever adopted by the natives outside the areas of intense romanization; in Gaul the Celtic language gave way to Latin, and in Britain it survived and evolved. The Picts of Caledonia remained a continuing threat. In 306 A.D. they penetrated Roman defenses only to be contained by Constantius Chlorus who died in York that same year. Another Pictish force reached London in 364 but was driven back by Theodosius the Great. From the fourth century the situation grew more critical for the Romans as Pictish and Scotti (Irish) tribes increasingly stepped up their attacks on Roman fortifications, so much so that before the end of the fourth century the Romans had to abandon Hadrian's Wall.

EXIT ROMANS, ENTER GERMANIC TRIBESMEN

Soon after the death of Emperor Constantine, the Roman Empire began to crumble. Franks and Goths crossed the Rhine in 406 A.D. attacking Rome's western territories, while fierce Huns from the east pounded away at her eastern frontiers. Rome began calling its military forces home from the peripheral regions of the Empire, leaving many of the out-lying provinces (including Britain) to look after their own defenses. The Romans pulled out of Britain in 407 A.D. leaving the island with no real provision for the future and exposed to invaders: fierce Picts from the north swarmed over the abandoned wall that Hadrian had built, and raiding Scotti from Ireland ravaged the western coastline.

Over the next several centuries the appearance of in-creasing numbers of Germanic tribesmen (Jutes, Angles, and Saxons) from the Continent, closely akin in language, reli-gion and customs, overran Britain, undoing the political and social institutions which the Romans had instituted. From what little is known about the period between the departure of the Romans and the Anglo-Saxon conquest, it is at times difficult to separate factual accounts from those that are mythical—many of which have been passed down in the Arthurian legends. Generally referred to as the "Dark Age," it bore witness to the disintegration of a remarkably civilized society and supporting institutions which the Romans had created on the island. Some historians believe the breakdown resulted from the impairment of strong central institutions when the Romans withdrew. They also believe it was caused by the restoration of the tribal system of independent petty kingdoms, which was accelerated by the arrival of increasing numbers of Germanic tribesmen whose social and political customs were in many ways similar to those of the natives.

According to tradition, a Celtic prince named Vortigern assumed command in eastern Britain after the last Roman ruler left the island, and he convened an armed force with which to push back the Picts and the *Scotti* (Irish). In 477 A.D. he appealed to Saxon chiefs Hengist and Horsa for military aid, and in exchange he allocated them territory.[9] He fell in love with Hengist's daughter, and to obtain her hand in marriage he surrendered Cantium (Kent) to Hengist, and to Hengist's son the land bordering on Hadrian's Wall. The Saxons, however, continued to be increasingly troublesome to deal with, so Vortigern is said to have fled to Wales where he built a stronghold at Mount Eryi (Snowdon). Vortigern's eldest son Gwerthevyr (sometimes identified as Vortiporius king of the *Demetae*) was much less appeasing to the Saxons than his father had been, and he waged several successful attacks against Hengist, "pushing the invaders back into the sea." It is also said that he killed the Saxon chief Horsa. After Gwerthevyr's death, Vortigern assumed the leadership of the west Britons; and, when the Saxons renewed their offensive, rather then march against them, he offered to negotiate. Thereupon, Hengist cunningly invited him and several hundred Britons to a banquet where he had ordered his servants to take Vortigern prisoner and slay the remainder of the guests. To get his freedom back, Vortigern had to turn over three of his richest territories to Hengist.

After the massacre of his kinsmen and the loss of his territories, Vortigern retired once again to his stronghold in Wales. At this point, tradition has it that Ambrosius Aurelius and Uther Pendragon returned to Wales from Armorica (Brittany) to avenge Vortigern's treacherous killing of their father some years before. Ambrosius was crowned king and became the leader of the resistance movement against the Saxons. He led an attack on Vortigern's stronghold, setting it ablaze and engulfing Vortigern and his family in the flames. At the time of Vortigern's death (*c.* 461 A.D.), much of the southeastern region of the island was in Anglo-Saxon hands and the core of the resistance movement had moved to Wales under Uther Pendragon. It is through him that the story enters the Arthurian cycle where the struggle against the Saxon is told through the magical world of heroic deeds and legends in which the tribal chief Arthur is transformed into the real King Arthur. Like the Continental Celts, the Britons were constantly seeking solidarity which invariably escaped them. Their Celtic world was crumbling: first it was the Roman invaders, then the Saxons. Although embittered and disillusioned, Britons still hoped for military success, and it is through the adventures of the legendary King Arthur that the final chapter of the great struggle between the Britons and their Saxon foe is told.

The earliest mention of Arthur occurs in the extant manuscript, *Gododin*, by the bard Aneurin which dates from the thirteenth century but is believed to contain passages from a much earlier text. The second allusion to Arthur comes in the *Historia Brittonum* which contains a blend of data from different writers, including the ninth century chronicler Nennius. Here, Arthur is described as *dux bellorum*, a war leader.[10] We are told that he fought a fierce campaign against the Saxons and won a great victory at Mount Badon (identified as Baydon Hill on the western border of Wessex) which the *Annals of Cambri* lists as the year 516 A.D. The victory at Mount Badon is also mentioned in Gildas' *De Excidio Britanniae* where the victorious leader is named Aurelius Ambrosius, leading many historians to suggest that Aurelius and Arthur were one and the same person.

Arthur and his contemporaries managed to halt the Anglo-Saxon expansion into the west until the middle of the sixth century; but, soon after 550 A.D., the Saxons defeated the Britons at Salisbury and pushed westward again. Twenty-seven years later a stunning defeat was handed to the Britons at Dyrham (577 A.D.), which delivered to the Saxons the strategic towns of Bath and Gloucester. The enemy had now reached the Severn valley, thereby cutting off Cornwall from Wales. It was at this point that several of the British tribes began to migrate. The *Cornovii* who had first settled on the Welsh borders were now in the Cornish peninsula and some crossed to find refuge in Brittany. The *Dunmonii*, whose home was Devon, also went to Brittany to the area of Saint-Malo and Dinan where they founded the kingdom of *Donmonia*. Meanwhile, some Welsh and northern Britain tribes found refuge in Finistere. According to Jean Markale,[11] Wales was then becoming overpopulated from the influx of refugees fleeing there from other parts of the island.

Several chieftains tried to pick up the pieces and organize anti-Saxon resistance, but they were continually engaged in fighting amongst themselves. The Anglo-Saxons were extending their domination over the native Britons: first in the kingdoms of Kent and Anglia and next in Devon. By the mid-seventh century Northumbria emerged out of the alliance of two Anglian kingdoms, Bernica and Deira, and was later extended to include all of the country from Yorkshire to the Lothians. Still later in the eight century, Northumbria was incorporated into the central Anglo-Saxon kingdom of Mercia which became important under the distinguished leader Offa. The various kingdoms continued to coalesce and around 927 A.D., under the leadership of Athelstan, there emerged the unified Anglo-Saxon kingdom of England.

But the Britons were determined to make one more attempt at overthrowing the Saxons. In 937, Howel Dda, king of south Wales and Powys, reunited the Britons by forming a coalition composed of Welshmen, Cornishmen, the men of Strathclyde and even Picts, Danes and Irishmen in order to drive out the Saxons. His forces were eventually defeated by the Saxon leader Athelstan. The area known as England was firmly in Saxon hands, but whether most of the Briton population was displaced by the new invaders is not known. From historical accounts, some of the Celtic-speaking peasantry were enslaved (a usual practice of the conqueror), others fled to the hilly regions in the west and the north, while yet others took refuge across the Channel in Brittany.

The Celtic world, which at an earlier date had encompassed most of northern and eastern Europe, was now confined to Ireland, Wales, the Scottish Highlands, Brittany and to a lesser degree in Cornwall, where the inhabitants held tightly to their Celtic language, customs and ways.

SCOTLAND

Scotland (to the Romans Caledonia) did not emerge into recorded history until Julius Agricola attempted to conquer it in 80–84 A.D. The *Picti* tribes, whom the Romans regarded as wild and barbaric, dominated the area from an early time. The Romans, however, were not successful in conquering the Picts, and Emperor Hadrian built a wall (120 A.D.) some twenty-two miles in length from the Solway to the Tyne to keep them from invading Roman Britain to the south.

The Picts were thought to be a pre-Celtic people by some early historians, among them Venerable Bede (*c.* 673–735), who regarded their language as different from Celtic. Later historians discounted this view and considered the Picts to be unquestionably Celtic, speaking a language (long lost) which was part Celtic and part belonging to some more ancient tongue, probably that of an indigenous people who were occupying the region when the Picts arrived. Little of the early Pictish tradition has survived; but, according to some sources their kinsmen, the Cruitins, ruled small kingdoms in northeastern Ulster (present-day counties Antrim and Down) up to the sixth century when they were brought under the overlordship of the expanding Ui Neill dynasty.

The Picts were the dominant tribes of Caledonia (sometimes referred to as Alba) until at least the fifth century when *Dal Riada* tribes from northeastern Ulster, who had earlier formed the Scotti (Irish) colony of Argyle, began expanding. As early as the third century, the *Dal Riada* began moving off their lands in western Munster and heading for the northeastern area of Ulster where they formed a new community among the Cruitin tribes. Shortly afterwards, a party crossed over to Alba where they established a colony in the peninsulas and islands that now make up Argyle in western Scotland. A century or so later the Argyle *Dal Riada* were joined by another party of their Kerry kinsmen under a leader named Fergus. Over the next century the *Dal Riada* battled the Picts steadfastly as they sought to expand beyond their original settlements to accommodate their ever-growing population. It was not until the fifth century, however, and with the aid of the Irish king Niall of the Nine Hostages, that the Picts were finally subdued along the western seaboard.

The *Dal Riada* in Alba remained closely linked, and some sources suggest tributary, to their kinsfolk in Ulster until 576 A.D. when they were granted autonomy at the Convention of Drimceatt. For the next two and a half centuries relations between the *Dal Riada* and the Pictish communities were relatively calm; however, near the end of the eighth century in the reign of Don Coirce, the Norsemen attacked and pushed the *Dal Riada* eastward from their settlements, and they in turn pushed the Picts further east and northeast. The windfalls of war changed several times before destiny ordained that the *Dal Riada* and the Picts be fused into one kingdom (Scotland). The driving force behind the unification was the *Dal Riada* king, Cinead (Kenneth) MacAlpin.

Now that the *Dal Riada* were the dominant people in Caledonia, except for the southeastern area ruled by the Anglos, the name Scotia Minor was applied to the area (Scotia had then been the name applied to Ireland). Later, the title Scotia was dropped completely from Ireland and became the exclusive name for the former Caledonia. The Gaelic language and influences came to prevail throughout the west and the Highlands; and, by the ninth century, the Picts had ceased to exist as an autonomous nation, though some aspects of their culture lingered on into the Anglo-Norman ascendancy.

---

[1] Gerhard Herm, *The Celts* (1977)

[2] Barry Cunliffe, *The Ancient Celts* (1997)

[3] T.G.E. Powell, *The Celts* (1960)

[4] Barry Cunliffe, *The Ancient Celts* (1997)

[5] Coinage did not develop among the British Celts until the second century B.C.

[6] As opposed to Goidelic, or Q-Celtic, the form spoken in Ireland

[7] Peter Berresford Ellis, *The Celtic Empire* (1990)

[8] Nora Chadwick, *The Celts* (1997)

[9] Jean Markale, *The Celts* (1993)

[10] Ibid.

[11] Ibid.

CHAPTER 5

CELTIC IRELAND

The historical period in Ireland did not begin until the fifth century A.D., when writing was first introduced with the coming of Christianity. Therefore, many of the stories passed down relating to Celtic invasions and the colonization of ancient Ireland have mythical overtones.

The oldest-surviving native historical record, believed to be the most reliable, is the *Annals of Tighernach*, a history of Ireland prepared in the late eleventh century A.D. at Clonmacnoise. During the twelfth century, a new book appeared in Ireland titled *Leabhar Gabhala* (Book of Invasions). In it were compiled the traditions of Ireland's ancient past, presumably both oral and written, detailing an account of the origins of the Celtic Irish, the various invasions and the formation of the monarchy. While it is classified as a work of mythology, there is undoubtedly much in it that is historically true. There are dim echoes of the Bronze and Iron Ages, and echoes of a society similar in many ways to the one the Romans found in Gaul in the first century B.C.

MYTHICAL IRELAND

The *Leabhar Gabhala* recounts, through a mythological character named Tuan, that the Partholan race took possession of Eirinn after the Deluge, and were sheep herders who cleared the island for cultivation and introduced the peculiar practice of fosterage[1] which survived in Gaelic Ireland until recent times. Next to arrive were Nemed and his followers who, according to Tuan, had sailed aimlessly for eighteen months on the Caspian Sea where many of them died of hunger before sailing to Ireland. Upon arrival, they fought the Formorians (believed to have been African pirates) for possession of the island. Following the Nemedians, there arrived the Erainn people: Fir Bolg, Fir Domnainn and Galiaian tribes (offshoots of the Continental Belgae)[2] who introduced a warlike aristocracy, including weapons of metal and a system of monarchy. These three groups did not vanish from the story like those before them; they left descendants, many of whom were enslaved by Ireland's last pre-Christian conquerors, the Gaels. Lending credence to this aspect of the legend is Ptolemy's account[3] confirming the widespread and dominant presence of Erainn, or Belgae, tribes throughout the island as early as the sixth century.

Tuan continued by describing the arrival of the Tuatha de Danann and the story of the famed battle at Moytura. Here, the De Dananns, described as a "beautiful people descended from the goddess Dana," met and overthrew the uncultured Fir Bolgs in a famed battle at Southern Moytura (on the Mayo-Galway border). King Eochaid of the Fir Bolgs was slain in this battle and King Nuada of the De Dananns had his hand severed by a Fir Bolg warrior named Sreng.

Because of this blemish King Nuada had to relinquish the kingship; for, under De Danann law, no king could rule who suffered a personal blemish. Consequently, the De Danann warrior Breas was given the kingship instead.

Breas (whose father happened to be a Formorian sea-pirate) ruled the De Danann tribes for seven years. During his reign he infuriated his people by standing idly by while the Formorians constantly came ashore from their stronghold on Tory Island (off the north coast of Ireland) to pillage and ransack the countryside. He was finally overthrown, and he fled to the Hebrides to seek his father's help. Breas and his father returned to Ireland with a large army only to be defeated by the De Dananns in a great battle at Northern Moytura in County Sligo. It was here that the most infamous Formorian chief of them all, Balor of the Evil Eye who ruled Tory Island off the northwest coast, was slain by a stone from the sling of his own grandson, the great De Danann hero Lugh. After the defeat many of the Fir Bolgs followed their Formorian allies to the Western Isles of Scotland, where they were oppressed by the Picts. They returned eventually to Ireland and, crossing the Shannon into Connacht, were received with open arms by their Fir Bolg kin and given lands by the celebrated Queen Meave.

An ancient tale in the *Yellow Book of Lecan* describes how the Gaels originated in Scythia (north of the Black Sea) and came to Ireland through Egypt, Crete and Spain. They were called the *Goidel* people, supposedly after a remote ancestor named Goidhal Glas who lived during the time of Moses. Goidhal's grandson, Niul, is believed to have married a Pharaoh's daughter, Scotia. Niul and Scotia, together with their people, were later banished from Egypt by a Pharaoh who became resentful of their growing power and success. After much wandering in search of a new home, they settled in Spain. There they heard stories from Phoenician traders of a green and misty isle to the north, which they took to be the Isle of Destiny foretold to them by Moses. Their leader Milesius sent his uncle, Ith, on a journey to find out more about this place. Ith did not return. The De Dananns, suspecting the motive for his visit, had him murdered.

Following Milesius' death, his wife (Scotia) and eight sons with their families and followers set sail for Ireland. As they neared the southwestern coast a dreadful storm overtook them, dispersing their fleet. Many in the flotilla, including five of Milesius' sons, were lost at sea. Those who survived made it ashore only to meet stubborn resistance from the De Danann natives. In due course they prevailed, conquering the De Dananns in a great battle at Taillte in County Meath where the De Dananns agreed that the sons of Mil should rule the land between them. *Eber* was given the southern half of the land; *Eremon* the northern half. *Ith's* son, *Lughaid*, was given the southwestern corner of Munster, and to the children of *Ir* went the northeastern corner of Ulster. In time, a dispute arose between the followers of *Eber* and *Eremon*. *Eremon* was victorious and, hence, through him was established the lineage and succession to the overlordship of the Gaels in Ireland. Another version has the land divided between *Eogan Mor*, alias *Mug Nuadat*, and Conn and tells of the struggle for supremacy between the two, which ended in the battle of Mag Lena when *Eogan* was slain by Conn.

Much of what is recounted in the mythical stories of Ireland's Celtic invasions and epic past would undoubtedly fail serious critical analysis. However, combined with archaeology and folklore, these mythical stories provide a key to unlocking a genuine long-lost history—however distorted by the passage of time—and help somewhat in unraveling the real story of ancient Ireland and from whence the various colonists originated.

ARCHAEOLOGICAL SOURCES

As the history of ancient Ireland was not recorded in written form until Christian times, the only earlier written references are those provided by Greek and Latin writers and geographers. But in Ireland, as elsewhere, there is a history predating written records, found in burial mounds, in artifacts from archaeological excavations and in the tales passed down orally from generation to generation. From such data it is observed that Ireland shared in the many stages of progress, from the various stone ages through those of copper, bronze and iron.

Archaeological sources acknowledge that the first human visitors to Ireland arrived eight thousand years ago. They were Mesolithic people who migrated across the North Channel from Scotland after the last Ice Age. The first "Irishmen" were a small, dark-featured people, most likely from the Mediterranean region, who had earlier migrated northward across Europe when the ice caps receded after the last Ice Age. Little is known of them except that they lived close to lakes and rivers. They left no clues as to a settled life—neither dwellings nor burial sites—only some charcoal traces of their campsites and some flint tools, mostly found in the northeastern region of Ulster.

Four thousand plus years later, a Neolithic race settled in Ireland. Their forebears had earlier transformed human survival by discovering the benefits of tilling soil and domesticating wild animals. They had long since been driven westward out of the Middle East by the expanding population and arrived in Ireland around 3700 B.C., presumably by way of Gaul and Britain. They, too, were small and dark, and they also used stone tools. They were, however, more sophisticated than the Mesolithic people they displaced. They made flint arrows and stone implements for domestic need, used stone axes to clear cuttings in the forests, plowed, sowed and reaped, and lived in settled communities. But, their most spectacular legacies were in the monuments of colossal stones they raised where they buried their dead and, perhaps, where they worshiped their gods.

Over the next two thousand years, the island was settled by successions of new Neolithic Stone Age invaders. Some had intensely skillful and sophisticated cultures, as seen by the many megalithic tombs dotting the countryside, the most elaborate of which is Newgrange in County Meath. Newgrange, built about 2500 B.C. around the time of the Egyptian pyramids, suggests a people with at least the sophistication of the pyramid-builders. In Carrowkeel in County Sligo, atop the Bricklieve Mountains, the ruins of another megalithic tomb, less imposing than Newgrange but nonetheless astounding, offers the visitor a glimpse into the distant past at what living may have been like for those prehistoric settlers. Many other smaller structures dot the Irish landscape attesting to the eccentricity of those ancient folk. Unfortunately, the Neolithic Stone Age people had no written language to pass on information about themselves. There is no record of what language

Entrance stone, megalithic tomb, about 2500 B.C., Newgrange, County Meath.

they spoke or how they worshiped their gods. The symbolism in their art is unclear, but their elaborate structures suggest a highly skillful people.

In time, the people who built Newgrange and Carrowkeel were overtaken by more invaders arriving and settling intermittently between 2100 and 1300 B.C. Archaeological discoveries confirm a new form of burial that was introduced during this period. Single-burial graves replaced the great stone communal tombs of the Neolithic people. Skeletons recovered show a round-headed people of a racial type new to Ireland. Gracefully decorated pottery of the period shows no continuity with anything of an earlier age in Ireland. These are referred to as the Beaker people (so called for their pottery style).

The Bronze Age began in Ireland around 1500 B.C., and with it came the arrival of a new wave of emigrants known to the archaeologists as the Urnfielders because they buried their dead in urns in flat cemeteries. They arrived from the Alpine region of Europe, probably through Britain, and are believed to have spoken an early form of Celtic. They are also believed to have possessed many of the traits and characteristics analogous to those of the later Celts, which would make them the first Celts to settle in Ireland.

CLASSICAL REFERENCES

The earliest geographical description of Ireland was prepared in the second century A.D. by Claudius Ptolemy,[4] a Greek astronomer and geographer from Alexandria. His original manuscripts have not survived, but a Latin version of his

Geography surfaced in the fifteenth century. It contained no actual map of Ireland, but lists latitude and longitude locations of estuaries, offshore islands, surrounding bodies of water, and tribal settlements. Many historians, including Thomas F. O'Rahilly[5] (1946), maintain that Ptolemy could not have been describing the Ireland of his own time when he prepared his *Geography*, as he made no reference to the *Laighin* colonists who are believed to have settled the island as early as 300 B.C. Nor did he make reference to the Gael settlers who are believed to have arrived around 150 B.C. or later. It is thought that he relied heavily upon the work of a geographer or traveler of a much earlier period, believed to be the lost work of Maximus of Tyre (325 B.C.). Maximus' work was derived from the lost *Periplus of Pytheas* of Massilia (*c.* 530 B.C.), the earliest known Greek geographer to have visited the Pretanic Islands, which he named for its inhabitants the *Picti.*

Many of the tribal names shown in Ptolemy's work can be positively identified. Names, such as *Menapii, Darini, Iverni* and so on, confirm the widespread and dominant presence of the Erainn or Belgae tribes at the time. Poseidonius (*c.* 135–50 B.C.) a Syrian historian and philosopher also wrote about Ireland, as did Strabo (64 B.C.–24 A.D.), a Greek geographer. Poseidonius' information on Ireland is vague and dubious. He mentions that the Irish were cannibals and fiercer than the inhabitants of Britain, but that the Iberians were cannibals as well. Strabo added little to Poseidonius' comments except that he thought that Ireland was to the north of Britain and, therefore, must be colder. Needless to say, the Roman knowledge of Ireland was just as imprecise. Pliny the Elder (*c.* 23–79 A.D.) mentions Ireland but his source, Marcus Vipsanius Agrippa (64–12 B.C.), had calculated Ireland to be four times the size it actually was.

THE EMERGENCE OF CELTIC IRELAND

The first Celtic-speaking tribes are believed to have arrived in Ireland about 600 B.C. in what is referred to as the Hallstatt era. They were followed by waves of other invaders, the main thrust of whom arrived in the later La Tene era sometime between the third and first centuries B.C. They poured onto the island from Gaul, Iberia and neighboring Britain. There were tribes from two main stems of the Continental Celts—the Belgae[6] originating in northern Gaul, and the Gaels from southern Gaul and the northern seaboard of the Iberian Peninsula—fleeing from the Roman legions who were advancing across Europe. By the time Julius Caesar had completed his conquest of Celtic Europe in the first century B.C., the beginning of the end of Celtic society on the Continent had arrived. The imperial armies of Rome next invaded Britain, and again the Celts capitulated. Only in Ireland, untouched by the Romans, would Celtic culture unfold and flourish, similar in many ways to what it had been in the centuries before the first Roman legions marched across the Alps to transform the face of Europe.

Native historical renditions of traditions mention four waves of Celtic invaders of Ireland in pre-Christian times: the *Priteni* who were the first to colonize the island; next the Belgae who invaded Ireland from northern Gaul and Britain; then the *Laighin* tribes, who came from Armorica (present-day Brittany) and may have invaded Ireland and Britain more or less simultaneously; and lastly the Gaels who reached Ireland from either northern Iberia or southern Gaul.

FIRST WAVE: *PRITENI* COLONISTS

The *Priteni* tribes (Ireland and Britain were known to the early Greeks as the Pretanic Islands) are believed to have arrived sometime after 700 B.C. Their descendants in Ireland became the *Cruitin* tribes, later living alongside the powerful *Dal Riada* (Belgae tribes) that dominated northeastern Ulster up to the ninth century A.D. The Romans, who never fully succeeded in conquering them in northern Britain, referred to them as the *Picti*, meaning "painted people."

SECOND WAVE: *EUERNI* COLONISTS

The second wave were the *Euerni*, or *Erainn*, belonging to the Belgae people of northern Gaul, who began arriving about the sixth century B.C. They called their new home *Eueriio*, which would later evolve through the old Irish *Eriu* to *Eire*, and from *Eire* to Ireland.

The Erainn, more commonly referred to in contemporary references as the Fir Bolgs, claimed descent from the god *Daire* through his son *Lughaid*; and, the Fir Bolgs preserved traditions which told how their ancestor *Lughaid* had led an army from Britain and conquered Ireland. The significance of this legend concerning *Lughaid* is that it points out that the Erainn, according to their own traditions, came to Ireland from Britain.[7] From Ptolemy's account of Ireland (*c.* 325 B.C.),

*Beehive oratory where the early Irish Christian monks went into the
wilderness to pray (6ᵀᴴ–7ᵀᴴ century A.D.).*

there is good reason to believe that the *Erainn* tribes were
then the most widespread and predominant on the island.

After the beginning of the La Tene era, the *Euerni* were
followed by other Belgae colonists who spoke a Brythonic,
that is, a P-Celtic dialect; but, after they settled in Ireland,
they took on the old *Goidelic*, that is Q-Celtic language. They
contributed greatly to their adopted country with their art
forms: swords, torques and vessels very similar to those produced on the Continent. Yet, there is little evidence that their
technological capabilities had any affect on the archaic lifestyle of the natives. They seem to have set up very few
oppidum-like hill settlements, common in Britain and the
Continent at the time. Instead, they made do with the natives'
style of dwellings: rudimentary circular, beehive-shaped
stone houses built without mortar.

Several offshoots of the Belgae, or Fir Bolg colonists can be identified: the *Menappi* in Wicklow, the *Dal Riada* in west Antrim and the *Dal Fiatach* in east Ulster. Norman Mongan (1995) maintains that many of the present name places in Ireland containing syllables such as mong, muin, maine, managh, monach, manach, mannog, etc., attest to the presence of the Fir Bolgs in the area at some stage.

THIRD WAVE: *LAIGHIN* COLONISTS

The third wave of colonization is believed to have taken place sometime about 300 B.C. They were the *Laginians* or, according to their own tradition, Gauls who came to Ireland from Armorica. Their name association with *Laighi*, the ancient name for Leinster, suggests that this was where they first settled. Another branch of the same people was the *Galioin* (or *Gailenga*) who settled in an area north of Dublin and Meath. Eventually the *Galioin* extended their power to northwestern Connacht and, in the process, forced many Fir Bolg tribes into the remoter parts of the province. One can still see, in the remoter areas of western Ireland, the remains of many great stone forts built by the Fir Bolgs in their defense against the *Galioins*. In the *Tain Bo Cuailnge*, there is mention of three thousand *Galioins* serving under Ailill and Meave in their expedition into Ulster against King Conchobar. Within a few generations, they established themselves in northern Connacht, where in County Sligo their descendants included the O'Hara and O'Gara families. The strength of the *Laginians* was uppermost in south Leinster where they remained the dominant power well into historic times. They made little impact in Munster or in Ulster, suggesting that their occupation was limited to parts of present day Leinster and Connacht. Like the Belgae, the *Laginian* tribes were linguistically P-Celts, and had kinsmen in Britain.

ARRIVAL OF THE GAELS

The last major Celtic settlement in Ireland took place sometime between 150–50 B.C. These people have been identified as the Gaels (sometimes referred to as the Milesians) who, according to tradition, fled Roman incursions into southern Gaul. These were Iron Age Celts, and their dominance over the island was to last well over a thousand years. The ancient manuscript *Leabhar Gabhala* has them landing at two locations—Kerry in the south and the Boyne estuary in the east. Those who landed through the Boyne estuary pushed the earlier *Laginian* settlers from their land in north Leinster and established their kingship at Tara. The southern Gael invaders had no fixed location in the beginning; instead, they pushed inland moving from one district to another until eventually they made Cashel their headquarters.

Gael subjugation of all the native Fir Bolgs and *Laighin* tribes was, according to O'Rahilly (1946), still incomplete as late as the beginning of the fifth century A.D. The *Ulaid* still ruled Emain and were challenging the midland Gaels for supremacy. It was only in 516 A.D. that the conquest of the midlands was complete when "the Plain of Mide" was wrested from the *Laighin*.

THE MELTING POT

Legendary accounts abound telling of conflicts and battles between the north Leinster Gaels and their *Laighin* neighbors. A poem written by Mael-Mura of Othain in 887 A.D.[8] tells of *Laighin* tribes rebelling against the Gael rulers of the Midlands. They captured Tara, slew the Gael king, Fiachu, and installed their own leader Ellium-mac-Conrach as king instead. Fiachu's son, Tuathal-Techtmar, then assembled an army of 60,000 and with the aid of Fiachra-Cassin (described as a pre-*Goidel* leader and a faithful ally of the Gaels in the early days of their conquest) marched on Tara against Ellium and regained the kingship for himself. Ellium was killed in the battle and his tribal allies (*Ligmuini*, *Galioin*, Fir Bolg and *Domnainn*) were defeated and reduced to subsidiary status. Tuathal, we are told, was perpetually at war with rebellious vassal tribes, particularly the *Attacotti*, during his forty-year reign as king. He was at last slain himself by his successor Nial who, in turn, was killed by Tuathal's son. It was at this point that the half-legendary, half-historical figure Conn of the Hundred Battles appeared from west of the Shannon (where he was king of the area then known as *coiced-Ol-nEcmacht*) to establish the kingdom of *Midhe* (Meath) with Tara as its capital. He then laid claim to the high kingship of Ireland which brought a challenge from the king of Munster, Eoghan Mor (nicknamed Mogh Nuadat). Then both men agreed to divide the island between them: Conn was given all the territory north of a line between Dublin and Galway, and Mogh received all the territory south of that line.

Conn was succeeded in the kingship by his son Art who, in turn, was succeeded by his son Cormac (*c.* 250 A.D.). During his kinship, he had to contend with the autocratic Finn MacCool and his warrior militia group known as the *Fianna*. According to the annalists, Finn and his followers had acquired great prestige and were extending their sphere of influence over the whole of Ireland except Ulster. Somewhat disturbed at what was developing, Cormac set about curtailing their power and prestige. Cormac is remembered as a great king. The *Book of Ballymote* describes him as "a noble, illustrious king . . . the world was replete with all that was good in his time: the food and the fat of the land, and the gifts of the sea were in abundance in this king's reign. There was neither woundings nor robberies in his time, but everyone enjoyed his own, in peace."[9] The *Book of Leinster* tells how Galls, Romans, Franks, Saxons, Caledonians and other foreigners would call upon him to seek his wisdom and counsel. Three great literary works are attributed to him. The first, *Teagasc an Riogh* (Instructions of a King), is set in the form of a dialogue between Cormac and his son Cairbre whom he was preparing to assume the kingship. The second, *The Book of Acaill*, is a code for criminal law forming part of the Irish Brehon Laws. The third great work attributed to Cormac, *The Psaltair of Tara,* is known only by the frequent references to it by ancient writers. Cormac's literary work would appear to corroborate the fact that there was a considerable amount of scholarly enlightenment in the Ireland of the third century A.D. Cormac died in 267 A.D., more than a century and a half before St. Patrick arrived; but, there is a tradition that he had become a Christian before his death and, inspired by his new faith, had made a dying wish to be buried at *Ros-na-Riogh* facing the east, and not with the other pagan kings at *Brugh-na-Boinne*.

EMERGENCE OF THE *CONNACHTA* DYNASTY

It was from Conn's descendants that the *Connachta* dynasty emerged in the Midlands. They were an ambitious and expansive people who were not content with simply ruling their Meath kingdom. At an early period some pushed westward across the River Shannon, made themselves master of what is the present-day province of Connacht, and, in doing so, subordinated the Fir Bolg and *Laighin* tribes long-established in the territory of *coiced-Ol-nEcmacht*. By the seventh century *coiced-Ol-nEcmacht* had been renamed *coiced-Connachta;* and, the term *Connachta*, first applied to Conn's descendants in Meath, was now more narrowly applied to emulate the status of the Gael rulers of *coiced-Connachta* from which emerged the powerful *Ui Briuin* dynasty and their O'Conor descendants.

EMERGENCE OF THE *UI NEILL* DYNASTY

Another of Conn's descendants was the remarkable Niall Noigiallach (Niall of the Nine Hostages) who reigned at Tara from 380 to 405 A.D. and whose descendants evolved into the *Ui Neill* dynastic clan. His father was Eochaidh Mugmedon who was king of Connacht towards the end of the fourth century A.D., and the clan stronghold was at *Durna Shelca*, near

Carn Froach[10] in County Roscommon. Eochaidh's grandfather was Cormac MacArt who, himself, was grandson of Conn.

Mugmedon had five sons: Brian, Ailill, Fiachra, Fergus and Niall. The mother of the first four was Mongfionn; Niall's mother was Carthann, daughter of a British king. According to legend, Carthann gave birth to Niall out on the "plain of Tara" while being pursued by a jealous Mongfionn. It is told that "she did not dare take the child with her; she left it there exposed to the birds. And none of the men of Ireland dared take it for fear of Mongfionn, so great was her magic power and so great the dread she inspired." Then the bard Torna came and rescued the infant revealing to him his destiny: ". . . Seven and twenty years you will rule over Ireland and you will be heir to Ireland forever."

When Mugmedon became high king in 358, the Connacht kingship went to Mongfionn's brother Criomhthan. Mongfionn, resentful of that fact, poisoned her brother so that her son Brian could be crowned. But Niall, his father's favorite, was made king instead; and, only after he became high king did Brian accede to the kingship of Connacht. Brian was killed in a battle near Tuam by his nephew, Daithi,[11] who then became king and ruled Connacht until he, in turn, assumed the high kingship in 405.

During his monarchy, Niall proved to be a formidable raider. He made numerous incursions into Caledonia, Britain and Gaul from which he carried back many hostages and much loot. On one of his expeditions he captured the boy Succat, who later became known to the world as St. Patrick, and carried him back to Ireland where he was sold into slavery to a chieftain named Milcho in Antrim. While on an expedition in Gaul (404 A.D.), Niall was ambushed and killed by one of his own countrymen: Eochaid, son of Enna Ceannselaigh, king of Leinster. Upon his death, his nephew, Daithi became high king and he, too, embarked on foreign forays for loot and hostages. Tradition has it that Daithi was the last of the pre-Christian kings.

Two of Niall's sons, Eoghan and Conall, invaded Ulster where they shared the lands they captured, with Eoghan founding the family of Tir Owen, and Conall the family of Tir Conaill. From then on, Ireland was no longer the land of the "five fifths" but was divided into seven kingdoms: Connacht, Munster, Leinster, Meath, *Airghialla* (Vassals of the East), *Ailech* (northwest Ulster) and *Ulaidh*, the remains of the former kingdom of Ulster on the Antrim coast. Niall's dynasty of *Ui Neill* continued to dominate in Ireland until the early part of the eleventh century during which time the high kingship alternated between the southern and northern branches of the clan. It wasn't until the twelfth century when the O'Conors, heirs to the *Ui Briuin* dynasty in Connacht, assumed the high kingship that the *Ui Neill* declined in power.

SOVEREIGNTY AND COEXISTENCE

Most pre-Gael tribes, collectively referred to as Fir Bolgs irrespective of their ethnic origins, remained in place forming the basis for the future society which would be dominated by the less numerous but more powerful Gaels. Verse passed down from the *fili*[12] affirms that tribes from the Gael, Fir Bolgs and *Laighin* peoples coexisted and intermarried. In his introduction to *Leabhar-I-Eadhra* (1980), Lambert McKenna, S.J. mentions that the *fili*, who were also genealogists, tell us of

71

the existence of two distinct kinds of ruling families in early Ireland. To the first kind belonged the families of the conquering Gaels who had established themselves as ascendancy powers. To the second were the leading families of the other races, such as the Fir Bolg and *Laighin* peoples who, although demoted to the level of tributary folk in many instances, were allowed to carry on a certain measure of control and freedom within their communities. Their chieftains, many of whom were men of wealth and influence, were often granted noble ancestry linking them to the ruling Gael families.

The early annalists tell us that Fir Bolg people survived as distinct tribes well into early historical times. In Connacht, Fir Bolg tribes such as the *Ui Maine, Conmhaicne,* and others farmed alongside the *Ui Fiachrach* and *Ui Briuin* families of the ascendancy Gaels. In Leinster, the Fir Bolg tribes were the *Ui Failige, Ui Bairrche* and *Ui Enechglaiss,* to mention but a few. In Ulster and in Munster, many tribes can be identified whose pedigrees can be traced to the Fir Bolgs. Likewise, tribes of the *Laighin* people flourished alongside their Gael masters. In the Midlands, they entered the service of the Gaels who assigned them "sword-land" in return for their services and tribute. *Laighin* tribes (*Gailing,* for example) also aided the Gaels in their conquest of Connacht, and were rewarded with territory in Mayo where the barony of Gallen preserves their name.

The flow of invaders was continuous over many centuries which, with the inevitable assimilation, has made it somewhat difficult to distinguish with certainty which tribe belonged to which people. Many of the earlier colonists were reduced to subsidiary tribes as the Gaels came to dominate. Others, powerful enough to maintain a substantial degree of sovereignty within their well-established territories, coexisted with the new rulers.

Coexistence didn't necessarily mean social equality. The *Book of Genealogies* (a work of genealogical treatise) compiled in 1650 by Sligo native MacFirbis, describes some unflattering characteristics given to the Fir Bolg and *Laighin* tribes. They were spoken of in demeaning terms while their Gael masters were heaped with praise. Of the Gaels it was said that, "Everyone who is white of skin, brown of hair, bold, honorable, daring, prosperous, bountiful in the bestowal of property, wealth, and rings, and who is not afraid of battle or combat, they are the descendants of Milesius of Erinn." The *Laighin* on the other hand were judged as, "Everyone who is fair-haired, vengeful, large, and every plunderer; every musical person, the professors of musical and entertaining performances, who are adept in all Druidical and magical arts, they are the descendants of the Tuatha de Danann." The Fir Bolgs were awarded the least flattering comments and were said to be, "Everyone who is black-haired, who is a tattler, guileful, tale-telling, noisy, contemptible; every wretched, mean, strolling, unsteady, harsh, and inhospitable person; every slave, every mean thief, the disturbers of every council, and every assembly, and the promoters of discord among the people, these are the descendants of the Fir Bolgs."

---

[1] In Celtic culture, fostering was common. Children would be fostered in the home of a druid, scholar or monk from about the age of seven in order to be educated.

[2] Historically, the Fir Bolg, Fir Domnainn and Galiaian can be equated with the *Dumnonii* of Britain who gave their name to Devon and to the *Domnonia* in Brittany.

[3] Believed to have been derived from the lost work of Pytheas of Massilia, *c.* 530 B.C., the earliest known geographer to have visited the area

[4] Ptolemy's *Geography*

[5] Thomas F. O'Rahilly, *Early Irish History and Mythology* (1946)

[6] Also referred to as the Eurerni, Belgae, *Menapia* and Fir Bolg

[7] Thomas F. O'Rahilly, *Early Irish History and Mythology* (1946)

[8] Ibid.

[9] Jean Markale, *The Celts* (1993)

[10] Carnfree

[11] Genealogists don't all agree on Daithi's relationship to Brioin. To some he was Brioin's son, to others he was Brioin's grandson.

[12] The ancient poets

CHAPTER 6

INSTITUTIONS AND WAY OF LIFE

The most comprehensive insight into the institutions and way of life in early Celtic society is passed down mainly from early Irish literary records wherein a large number of ancient law tracts relate detailed rules on a multitude of topics. There are earlier references on the subject from classical writers such as Caesar and Posidonius and, although less complete, they reveal many similarities between the way of life of the Continental Celts of the pre-Roman period and that of the Celts of Ireland in the early historical period. Considering the Irish Celts were a branch of the Continental mainstream, it is expected that they brought with them into the land of their adoption the mythology and customs of their homeland. Tacitus, writing at the end of the first century A.D., comments on how the Irish and the Britons were akin in many respects as far as customs and law went; and, for many centuries, the descendants of Irish colonists who settled in western Scotland preserved the customs, language and way of life brought there from Ireland by their ancestors. Therefore, the Irish model yields a reliable picture of what Celtic society was generally like in early times.

SOCIAL GROUPING

The social structure of Celtic Ireland was similar in many ways to Celtic Gaul and Britain in pre-Roman times, in that the island was divided into many tribal kingdoms based on family ties. A group of families occupied a division of land called a *tuath* within which the members equally owned the land. The members of the *tuath*, collectively known as the *deirbhfine*, consisted of all relations in the male line of descent for five generations. Included were a man's sons, his father's brothers, his grandfather's brothers and so on—all sharing alike in the family's belongings and privileges, achievements and misfortunes. Each *tuath* was presided over by a chieftain elected by its freemen (who alone had that privilege) from among the many eligible members of the ruling family. The king had certain delegated powers which included leading the army in time of war and representing the *tuath* in time of peace, but did not include making or enforcing the laws, which belonged to an assembly of freemen. Several *tuaths*, when allied together, made up a local kingdom which was ruled by an over-king. Local kingdoms, in turn, formed confederate alliances ruled by a provincial king.

TRIBAL RELATIONSHIPS

Celtic Ireland had a well-developed and complex tribal culture consisting of a highly codified legal system which regulated relationships within and between classes, families, larger kin-groups and inhabitants of *tuaths*. The early Irish law tracts tells us that society within the *tuath* was precisely defined. Below the *ri tuaithe*[1] was an aristocracy composed of the noble ranks whose status was measured partly by the number of their *celi*.[2] In early Irish law, clientship was known by the Gaelic term *ceilsine*. Beneath the aristocracy were the freemen (*boaire*), persons who belonged to the franchise-holding classes whose property had a value of at least twenty-one *cumals*.[3] Also included were the learned, certain skilled craftsmen and, alone among the musician class, the harpists. Beneath the *boaire* were the nonfree who constituted the majority of the *tuath* members. "Nonfree" did not mean slaves only, though there were slaves. The nonfree grouping were persons who did not have the legal rights of the freemen. They had no property or possessions; they were tenants, laborers, herdsmen, inferior craftsmen, squatters and interlopers from other territories. Agreements were transacted collectively on behalf of the community, as all *deirbhfine* property was communal. Members were given only limited rights. Leadership of the *tuath* belonged to members of the great families. Noblemen of lesser rank would attain at most the position of retinue leader. Mastery of an art or craft enabled a man to climb the social ladder. There were no towns or centralized authorities.

Rules for land tenure, set forth in the *Brehon Laws*, describe five different ways persons or families could have utility of land: in theory, the land belonged to the tribe through collective ownership. It is thought that in pre-historic times land was all common property; but, over time the concept of private ownership, for select classes, made its way into the system. The king or chief had a portion for his own use for a lifetime or for as long as he remained chief. Upon his retirement or death, the title went to his successor, be it his kin or a non-family member. This was known as descent by *tanistry*. Another portion of the *tuath* land was held privately by freemen (nobles and professional men) who had come in various ways to acquire land. Title to privately owned property customarily passed to an heir. The nonfree *tuath* members were without ownership of land. They were the tenant class and they rented their pieces of land from the *boaire* or freemen class. When a tenant died, his farm did not go to his children but reverted to the *fine* or sept, whereupon the whole of the land belonging to the sept was *gavelled* (redivided) among all the male adults of the sept including the deceased's adult sons. The next portioning was that of arable tribe-land which formed by far the largest part of the *tuath* property, and which was held in common by the tributary families. The remainder, non-arable or waste land, was community land which every free man shared for grazing and other purposes. Between common ownership and private ownership there was an intermediate link where, in some cases, land was owned by a family (instead of a family member) and remained in the same family for generations. A peculiar form of family ownership was that known as the *Gelfine* system, under which four families or groups of related persons held four adjacent tracts as a sort of common property subject to a contractual agreement.[4]

BREHON LAWS

Law formed an important component both in public and in private relationships in ancient Ireland. The native legal system was outlined in a body of laws now referred to as the *Brehon Laws*, derived from the Irish term "brehon" which was applied to the lawgiver. These laws governed most of Ireland for many, many centuries until they were replaced by English administrative law at the beginning of the seventeenth century. The most important of the codes are contained in two volumes: the *Senchus Mor* (chiefly concerned with Irish civil law) and the *Book of Acaill* (concerned with what is now known as criminal law). Few, if any, of the Brehon codes were enacted through a legislative process similar to what is common today; instead, they were precedents and commentaries of venerable law-givers of earlier times and were executed not through some executive means but through the moral persuasion of public opinion.

Brehons were an influential class and those attached to chiefs had free lands which, like the profession itself, remained in the family for generations. Those not so attached lived simply on the fees received from rendering decisions, said to be one-twelfth of the property in dispute, or of the fine in case of an action for damages. A brehon was not a judge in the strict sense of the word; he was more of a legal expert who devoted himself to arbitrating disputes, and at times to advising his clients. Brehons studied extensively to master the complicated rules and obscure technical terms embodied in the volumes of legal codes from which they rendered their judgements.

ADMINISTRATION OF JUSTICE

In ancient Celtic Ireland, every offense was against the individual, as there was no national form of authority to make laws and accordingly no offense against the state could be entered. In Ireland in those times there were no law enforcement officers, so any attempt to seek redress from the offender had to be initiated by the injured party or his friends. According to Joyce, "The injured party, having no civil authority to appeal to, might at once, if he chose, take the law into his own hands. But though this was sometimes done, public sentiment was decidedly against it, and the long-established custom was to refer all such matters to the arbitration of a brehon. Accordingly, the person injured sued the offender in proper form, and if the latter responded, the case was referred to the local brehon. . . ." If the offender refused to respond to the complaint, or if he withheld payment after the case was decided against him, the plaintiff could then seize the cattle or other assets of the defendant, but only when he had proceeded by *distress*, a course of action spelled out in the Brehon codes.

The death penalty was imposed for certain crimes, though never as the result of a judicial process before a brehon where punishment was a fine (*eric*). The *eric* consisted of two parts: the first was compensation for the injury based upon the severity of the injury; the second, described as honor-price, was meted out according to the status or rank of the aggrieved party. When the death penalty was applied, the methods used to put criminals to death varied: drowning (tied in a sack or with a heavy stone secured to the body), or hanging from a scaffold. Women who committed adultery were burned at the stake.

SELECTING LEADERS

The *ri tuaithe* (petty king) was elected to office by a gathering of the privileged classes who represented a minority assembly as it excluded the non-privileged members. All male descendants of a former king, extending to and including great-grandsons, were eligible to compete for the kingship spot. Primogeniture was not an advantage; superior military aptitude and leadership talent were the essential requirements. Much was expected of the person who occupied the highest office in the *tuath*. By present day standards, one could reason that it was a democratic system in a way. There were flaws, nonetheless, in the *modus operandi*. The rule precluding primogeniture succession often meant many rival contenders for the kingship, thus producing many disgruntled contenders believing that they were the better qualified and, therefore, had a more rightful claim.

The situation was further aggravated by a custom which prescribed that a family whose contention for the kingship had failed over four generations thereupon lost its noble status, privileges, power, prestige and its eligibility to seek election another time. Families faced with this plight stopped at nothing—murder, war or both—to avert the stigma this brought upon them. Fathers ended up fighting sons, sons fighting brothers, uncles and cousins, and so on. Family feuds were sparked off and lasted for generations. Feuds with neighboring families added to the hostilities; young warriors, determined to demonstrate their fighting qualities and suitability for kingship, led random raids into adjoining territories.

The inauguration or making of a king, after his election, was a splendid affair. When Cathal Crobhderg (O'Conor) was inaugurated king of Connacht at Carnfree in County Roscommon in 1201, the event was recorded by Donough O'Mulconroy, who was an eye-witness at the ceremony. What Donough wrote (reproduced below) illustrates the impressive ceremonial protocol and the courtly behavior of the Connacht nobles and their attendants at the inauguration of their king:

"This is the lawful form of inauguration of the king of Connaught, as it was established in the olden time, and ordained by St. Patrick on the day that he inaugurated Duach Galach, and on which occasion he was assisted by twelve bishops. And it is necessary that the successors of these bishops should be present at his inauguration, namely the successor of St. Patrick at Elphin, the successor of St. Bridget at Ballintuber, the successor of Dachonna of Asmacnerk (now Assylinn), the successor of St. Beo-Aedh of Ardcarn, the successor of Barry at Clooncorby (now Kilbarry), the successor of St. Colman of Mayom, the successor of St. Giallan of Moygillen, the successor of Bishop Sechell of Lough Salchern, the successor of St. Grellan of Creeve, the successor of St. Callin of Fenagh, the successor of St. Finian of Cloncraff.

"It was also ordained that the twelve dynasts or sub-chiefs of Connaught should be present at this inauguration, namely, O'Flannagan, O'Mulrenin, O'Finaghty and Mageraghty (who were called the four royal chieftains of the King of Connaught); O'Flynn, O'Hanley, O'Fallon, O'Beirne, O'Concannon, O'Heyne, O'Shaughnessy and O'Teighe, who was chief of the household of the King of Connaught.

"It was also required that the following chiefs should be present at his installation, namely, O'Rourke, O'Reilly, O'Hara and O'Gara, with their followers and MacDermot, chief of Moylurg.

"It is the privilege of O'Mulconroy to place the rod in the hands of O'Conor, the day on which he assumes the sovereignty of Connaught, and it is considered unlawful that any man should be along with the King on the carn except O'Mulconroy and O'Connaghten fronting O'Mulconroy, or more truly fronting O'Mulrenin, who kept the entrance of the carn.

"The King's clothing and arms were given to O'Mulconroy and his steed to O'Flynn the coarb of St. Dachonna, who was privileged to mount that steed from O'Conor's back. An ounce of gold was decreed to O'Connaghten as a perennial tribute, on condition of his repairing the carn when it required repairs. The following are the subsidies paid to the different chieftains of Sil Murray by O'Conor, King of Connaught. Twelve score milch cows, twelve score sheep, and twelve score cows to O'Flannagan, and the same number to Mageraghty and O'Mulrenin. The office of the High Steward to O'Conor was ceded to O'Flannagan, O'Hanley is the keeper of his hostages and he had the command of his fleet from Slieve-in-Iarain to Luinnech (Limerick) with all the perquisites thereupon belonging. MacBranan is henchman, and chief of his kerne, and the caretaker of his hounds. MacDockwra is his procurator-general who is bound to furnish light and bedding. It is the duty of O'Flannagan, O'Beirne and MacDockwra to guard the spoils of O'Conor, whenever he encamps to rest. MacBranan has the perquisites arising from O'Conor's marchership, from Curragh-Kinnetty (near Roscommon) to Kells in Meath; O'Flynn the marchership in the tract extending from Curragh-Kinnetty to Croagh Patrick, together with its stewardship.

"The chief command of O'Conor's fleet belongs to O'Flaherty and O'Malley. O'Kelly is the chief treasure of his precious stones, and all other species of treasure. MacDermot of Moylurg is his marshal; O'Teighe the chief of his household; O'Beirne his chief butler; O'Finaghty his chief doorkeeper; O'Mulconroy the recorder of all his tributes; MacTully his physician, and MacEgan his brehon (judge).

"Twenty-four townlands constitute the lawful patrimony of each of these eight chiefs, in payment of the offices they discharge for O'Conor. Forty-eight townlands, constituted the patrimony of each of his four royal chiefs, O'Flannagan, O'Mulrenin, Mageraghty and O'Finaghty, together with all dead Church lands.

"The chiefs tributary to O'Conor were those of Galenga Costello, Clann Cuan, Conmairne, Carra, and the two Leynies. In short, there was not a king, or royal heir, or chieftain of a cantred, or a district, or a hundred-cattled farmer of a townland from Assaroe to Luinne (Limerick) and from Uisnech in Meath to Inish-Boffenne, and from Lough Eren to Lough Deirgherc, who was not specially bound to attend with his forces at the hostings of O'Conor.

"The free states of Connaught are the following, namely, Ui-Briuin of Brefney, the Ui-Fiachrach of the Moy, and the race of Muiredhach, son of Fergus, and even of these, notwithstanding their freedom, two are bound to attend with their forces at the hostings of O'Conor, and to assist him in all his troubles and difficulties."[5]

WARFARE

Celtic society was isolated and beyond the influence of the civilized world in the centuries following the Gael ascendancy. Because of this, it continued to function as it had in Britain and Gaul prior to Roman influence. Celtic Irish lifestyle was rural, strongly tribal and loosely organized into largely autonomous communities, bound together by family ties and in marked contrast to the centralized and urban characteristic of Roman society. It was a heroic age that kept alive traditions which settlers had brought from their European homeland. Kings fought kings, warriors stole wives and massacred herds and flocks. Conflict flared mainly on issues of livestock where the rustling of cattle was a usual pretext for a call to arms. It was very much a society of aristocrats and Iron Age warriors with a culture akin to that of Homeric Greece.

On the whole, there was little impetus towards the creation of centralized political and administrative institutions because society had little use for them. Celtic society's strength and stability lay in a generally diffused body of social customs and laws enforced entirely within the context of closely-integrated neighborhood units. Political power, somewhat detached from this, was grounded not in social institutions but in tribal loyalties, in charismatic qualities of leadership, and in military skill.

---

[1] Petty king

[2] Clients

[3] A cumal equaled a female slave and she was worth four milch cows.

[4] P.W. Joyce, *A Social History of Ancient Ireland*, vol. 1 (1997)

[5] The text of Donnchadh O'Mulconroy's description of the inauguration ceremony of Cathal Crobhderg is from *MacDermot of Moylurg* by Dermot MacDermot (1996).

CHAPTER 7

DRUIDISM AND THE DRUIDS

The Celts of Gaul, Britain and Ireland practiced an ancient pagan faith called Druidism, akin to that practiced elsewhere by the Celts. Their chief gods were those of the Iron Age Celts, deities from a pre-Iron Age matriarchal system that personified the forces of nature. It was a religion governed by its priests who were called druids. The druids wielded immense power over their communities. Diodorus of Sicily wrote in the first century B.C. that, "Those men called by us philosophers and theologians are held in great honor by them; they call them druids . . . and no sacrifice may be performed without a druid present . . . for only they speak the language of the gods." Much about Druidism and its ancient practices and rituals remains shrouded in mystery because the druids wanted it that way—and no wonder, since only they knew "the language of the gods."

The information on the religious beliefs and practices of the pre-Christian Celtic people comes from a variety of sources (Greek and Roman texts), much of it in reference to

Celtic worship.

isolated facts with few references that provide a coherent account of Druidism as a whole. The most detailed accounts are those given by Caesar in his unflattering commentaries of Gaulish society.

There is, however, a body of knowledge on Irish Druidism, although to some extent nebulous. Ironically, it has come down by way of the ancient Irish monks who transcribed the oral accounts from earlier times. Not surprisingly, in the process of doing so, they interposed Christian allusions and modified many pagan features to fit Christian concepts. Early Welsh literature contains a certain amount of relevant material, but it was transcribed at a much later date than were the Irish renditions. As a result, it was even more influenced by Christian introspective. On the other hand, archaeological evidence for Celtic cults is generally more abundant from pre-Christian Gaul and Britain than from Ireland.

CELTIC DEITIES

According to Caesar, the Celts were to a great extent a religious people. Cunliffe tells us that the Celtic world was pervaded by a multiplicity of gods and goddesses of whom the names of 200 have been recorded. When Caesar wrote about the gods most commonly worshiped by the Gauls, he tried to correlate them with those of the Roman Pantheon: Mercury, Apollo, Mars, Minerva, etc. Mercury was the most popular, regarded as the inventor of all arts and presider over travel and commerce; Apollo turned away diseases; Mars controlled warfare; and Minerva protected industry and crafts. Celtic historian Nora Chadwick maintains that frequent efforts to

Seated god, 3ᴿᴰ–1ˢᵀ cent. B.C.; bronze.

match the deities mentioned by Caesar with the names of Celtic gods from Romano-Celtic inscriptions or early Celtic literature, have proved futile.

The poet Lucan named three Celtic deities—Teutates, Taranis and Esus—whom he says were appeased by human sacrifice: the victims of Teutates were to be drowned, those of Taranis burned, and those sacrificed to Esus hanged. Cunliffe translates Teutates to mean "the god of the tribe" from the Celtic *teuta* (tribe), Taranis to mean "a sky god" as the name was derived from the Celtic *taran* (thunder), and Esus as probably synonymous with Lugh, a widely revered deity of the Celtic world. Lugh's name is preserved in a number of places such as Lugudunum (Lyons) and Luguvallum (Carlisle), and also in Ireland where he was celebrated at the harvest feast of Lugnasad held on August 1.

Allusions to the Celtic gods in Irish literature are made in vague and general terms, as evident in the oath of the Red Branch: "I swear by the gods that my people swear by." Yet, there are many individual gods—some virtuous and some evil—that are known. Some have been identified with the gods of ancient Gaul; this is not surprising, considering many of the Celtic tribes who colonized Ireland (and Scotland) were from Gaul, and they naturally brought their traditions and mythology with them.

Among the Irish Celtic gods was Manannan Mac Lir whose name *Mac Lir* signifies "Son of the Sea." He is usually represented in the old tales as riding on the sea in a chariot at the head of his followers. Traditionally, he is supposed to have lived on the Isle of Man, where he was the first king. In Irish mythology he was an important god, being able, for example, to create storms to turn back invading ships. He is

91

associated with the Welsh deity Manawydan Fab Llyr. Another of the Irish deities, Dagda, whose name meant the "the good god," was a father-god and chief of the Tuatha de Danann. According to legend, Dagda always carried a gigantic club that had magical powers: one end of the club was destructive and was used to kill enemies, the other could heal the wounded and even revive the dead. There was also Lug, the god of arts and crafts, who was regarded as one of the more important gods. Legend has it that he killed the great warrior and Formorian chief, Balor of the Evil Eye, and led his Tuatha de Danann people to victory at the second battle of Moytura (present-day Sligo). He was akin to the British and Gaulish god Lugas, and to the Welsh god Lludd. In Irish Celtic mythology, Luchtine was one of a triad of craft gods; the other two, sometimes described as his brothers, were Goibhniu and Creidhne.

Among the oldest members of the Celtic pantheon were powerful goddesses, often grouped like their male counterparts in trinities. The Romans called them *matres* or *matronal*, and asserted that the highest honors were paid to them, including human sacrifice. There is also mention of hunting goddesses such as Arduinna, to whom the Ardennes owe their name; Belisama, who was also identified as Minerva; Damona, who was considered the goddess of war. There was in old Ireland, and in Gaul as well, a mother called Brigit who gained admittance into Christian sainthood as St. Bridget. Brigit is esteemed as one of the goddesses who was both a single goddess and a triple goddess. She was associated with healing, fertility, crafts, poetry and learning. According to one legend she was the daughter of Dagda. In Gaulish mythology Epona (meaning horse) was a horse-goddess and, as horses were of particular importance to the Celts, Epona was regarded as an important deity. Another Gaulish female deity was Ianuaria who was venerated at the sanctuary of Beire-le-Chatel in Burgundy. In Irish Celtic mythology Dana was a mother-goddess and the mother of the Tuatha de Danann. Morgen was a Druidic goddess according to Welsh mythology, and Nantosvelta according to Gaulish mythology.

Idol worship was not uncommon. In Celtic Ireland there was a great idol called *Cromm Cruach* at *Magh Slecht* near the present-day village of Ballymagauran in County Cavan. Some of the ancient manuscripts describe him as the chief idol of Ireland who, until St. Patrick's arrival, "was the god of every folk that colonized Ireland." Joyce mentions another remarkable idol in the western part of Connacht called *Cromm Dubh*, and Ulster had its own idol-god named *Kermand Kelstach*. Pillar-stones were worshiped in other parts of Ireland, as well as in Britain and on the Continent. The worship of water, as depicted in wells, is often mentioned in the early manuscripts. The *Book of Armagh*, among other annals, relates the story of St. Patrick who, on his journey through Connacht, came upon a well called *Slan* (meaning healing) which the pagan Celts worshiped as a god. They believed that a certain *fiath* (prophet) was buried beneath it in a stone coffin "to keep his bones cool from fire that he dreaded."[1]

PLACES OF WORSHIP

More impressive and convincing among classical references to Celtic Druidism are those which relate not to the gods, but to their places of worship. Although the Celts sometimes

Carved sandstone. Left, above: *Pillar, late 4ᵀᴴ cent. B.C.* Below: *Pillar, 3ᴿᴰ cent. B.C.* Right, above: *God with boar, 3ᴿᴰ cent. B.C.* Below: *Head, end of 1ˢᵀ cent. B.C.*

built temples for the worship of their gods, they very often used natural landscape locations as the center of their devotion. These are found frequently in sacred woods and near lakes and swamps. The most sacred grove in Britain was the one on Anglesey Island in northern Wales which Tacitus says was "devoted to barbarous superstition" and which Suetonius Paulinus and his Roman legions destroyed in 61 A.D. Some of the sanctuaries, it is told, reflected a ritual preoccupation with the natural environment. The poet Lucan in the first century A.D. tells of a sacred grove near Marseilles:

A grove there was, untouched by men's hands from ancient times, whose interlacing boughs enclosed a space of darkness and cold shade, and banished the sunshine from above. No rural Pan dwelt there, nor Silvanus, ruler of the woods, nor Nymphs; but gods were worshiped there with savage rites, the altars were heaped with hideous offerings, and every tree was sprinkled with human gore. On these boughs, if antiquity, reverential of the gods, deserves any credit, birds feared to perch; in those coverts wild beasts would not lie down; no wind ever bore down upon that wood, nor thunderbolt hurled from black clouds; the trees, even when they spread their leaves to no breeze, rustled among themselves. Water also fell there in abundance from dark springs. The images of the gods, grim and rude, were uncouth blocks, formed of felled tree-trunks. Legend also told that often the subterranean hollows quaked and bellowed, that yew trees fell down and rose again, that the glare of conflagration came from trees that were not on fire, and that serpents twined and glided round the stems. The people never resorted thither to worship at close quarters, but left the place to the gods. When the sun is in mid-heaven or dark night fills the sky, the priest himself dreads their approach and fears to surprise the lord of the grove.

Trees were also regarded as a quintessence of the divine. In Gaul and Galatia the oak, above all, was venerated; in Britain it was the yew; and in Ireland, the rowan. It was not until they came under Etruscan influence at the end of the Hallstatt period that the Celts gave their gods human shape. The wooden idols created by the wood-carvers prompted the poet Lucan to remark on them: "grim-faced god-images, coarsely hewn from rough tree trunks, bleached near shaded springs. . . ."

ROLE OF THE DRUIDS

In Celtic culture druids were priests who represented the most authoritative force in Celtic society. In all matters of dispute, druids alone judged and decided, fixing punishments and rewards where crimes had been committed, or where boundary and inheritance disputes arose. A person or persons failing to respect a druid's decision was expelled from public worship, regarded as the most humiliating punishment imaginable: "Those thus excommunicated count as godless criminals; all must avoid them and eschew any talk with them, lest the infection be passed on."

The druids enjoyed various benefits: they were exempt from tax and were not required to serve in the military. The privileges of the class attracted many pupils who would be required to spend twenty years studying the doctrine, committing everything to memory.

Gaul was the center of continental Druidism, and in Britain the chief center was at Mona (Anglesey). Gaulish druids were under one chief druid who held that position for life. He had supreme authority and met annually with other druids at a location in the territory of the *Crnutes*, considered to be the center of Gaul. There was no such institution in Ireland, although there were distinguished druids in various districts and attached to regional kingships.

DRUIDISM IN IRELAND

Druids in Ireland were, according to historian P.W. Joyce, the exclusive possessors of whatever learning was then known. They were not only druids in the precise interpretation of their role, but they were judges, prophets, historians, poets and even physicians. There were druids throughout Ireland, but their chief seat was at Tara, also the seat of the high kings of Ireland. Irish druids had the reputation of being great magicians, and for this they are written about most frequently by the early copyists. We are told that they could "raise Druidical clouds and mists and bring down showers of fire and blood; they could drive a man insane or into idiocy by flinging a magic wisp of straw in his face." According to some of the old historical legends, the outcomes of battles were sometimes determined, not so much by the gallantry of the warriors, as by the magical powers of the druids. Joyce points out that the *Tripartite of St. Patrick* and Adamnan's *Life of Saint Columba* refer to the druids and their magical powers, as do the historical tales. Tigernach and other annalists relate how before the Battle of Cul-Dremne (561 A.D.), fought between the northern and southern branches of the Ui Neill dynasty, Dermot (king of the southern Ui Neill and a Christian) called for the Druid Fraechan to make a protective magical *aire druad* (druid's fence) around the southern army. The druid's spell, however, collapsed when a warrior named Mag Laim from the northern side made a suicidal dash through the hexed line. The resulting effect was defeat and heavy casualties for Cormac's side, while Mag Laim was the lone casualty on the other side.

Druids were held as the intermediaries with the spirit world and as such had the power to safeguard people from the maliciousness of evil-disposed spirits; this, in fact, explains much of their sway over the people. Another important function was divination or the predicting of future events, practiced in connection with most important affairs and particularly with military expeditions. Queen Meave, before setting out on the *Tain* expedition, conferred with her druid to seek counsel and a foretelling of the future. He is said to have told her that "whosoever they be that will not return, thou thyself shalt certainly return." When Daithi was king of Ireland (405–428 A.D.), he ordered his druid to forecast events in his reign for the next year and was told, "Art thou asleep, O King of Erin and Alban (Scotland)?" And the king replied, "Why the addition to my title? I am not king of

Alban." To this, the druid answered that he had consulted "the clouds of the men of Erin," by which he found that the king would make a conquering expedition to Alban, Britain and Gaul, which he did soon afterwards.

A most important function of the druids was that of teaching. They were indeed the only educators, which greatly added to their influence. They were engaged to teach the children of kings and chieftains: both of King Laegaire's daughters were sent to *Cruachan* in Connacht to be taught by two druids. St. Columba, as a youngster, began his education under a druid. The chief druid of a king held a very influential position: he was the king's confidential adviser on important affairs. When King Conchobar mac Nessa of Ulster contemplated avenging the foray of Queen Meave of Connacht, he sought and followed the advice of his "right illustrious" Druid Cathbad as to the time and manner of the projected expedition. And on St. Patrick's visit to Tara, King Laegaire's proceedings were entirely regulated by the advice of his two chief druids, Lucetmail and Lochru.[2]

Producing insanity was the most dreaded of the sorcery powers attributed to the druids. Not only in pagan times, but well into the Christian era, insanity was believed to be often brought on by a spiteful magical source, usually the work of some druid. For this purpose, the druid prepared a "madman's wisp" (a wisp of straw or grass) into which he pronounced some offensive incantations before tossing it into the face of his victim, who at once became insane or idiotic.

DRUIDIC TEACHING AND PRACTICES

Gaulish (and probably British) druids taught about the immortality of the soul which was not a theory of reincarnation, but a belief based on the fact that when a person died he or she simply changed places or worlds. They held that there was constant exchanging of souls taking place between this world and the Otherworld—a death in this world meant a soul departing for the Otherworld, and a death in the Otherworld meant a soul arriving in this world. It was for this reason that the Celts were said to have mourned and celebrated death.

There is little evidence from available Irish sources to show that the Irish druids believed in immortality, or that the spirits of those who died were rewarded or punished in the Otherworld for their conduct in this one, or in fact that their spirits existed after death. There was a belief in a land of everlasting youth and peace which was described as beautiful beyond conception, always inhabited by fairies and called by various names. In ancient Irish romantic tales there are many descriptions of this heavenly place bearing a resemblance to each other, and of individuals who became immortal there.[3] Connla's (king of Ireland in the second century) son was carried off in a crystal boat to Fairyland by a fairy maiden before the eyes of his father and friends and was never seen on earth again.[4] The name *Tir Tairngiri* (meaning Land of Promise) is often mentioned, not only in the tales, but also in the Christian legends of the saints. Joyce mentions how St. Brendan prayed for some secure, delightful land remote from the haunts of men, and was told by an angel to go to *Tir Tairngiri*; thus, in search of this happy land, Brendan went on his celebrated voyage upon the Western Ocean.

Caesar alludes to human sacrifice as being part of the homage of the Gaulish druids. Others, Nora Chadwick among them, while acknowledging that human sacrifice was of great ritual significance to the Celts, take the position that it may have been practiced more commonly at times of communal danger rather than as part of regular ritual observance. There is no evidence that the Irish druids engaged in human sacrifice. The ancient Irish did practice a rite called the "Bull Feast" in choosing a future king, where "a white bull was killed, and one man ate enough of its flesh, and drank of its broth: and he slept under that meal; and a spell of truth was chanted over him by four druids: and he saw in a dream the shape and description of the man who should be made king. . . ."[5]

DRUIDIC RELIGIOUS OBSERVANCES

Celtic concepts of time are mainly from Irish literature which provides a detailed insight into the divisions of the year. Major Druidic religious observances focused on the solstices, equinoxes and moon phases. The end of the old year and the beginning of the new was marked by the greatest of the ceremonies, *Samhain*, observed on November 1. It was a time when the spirits of the dead could roam freely. It was a time when all the important communal acts, meetings and sacrifices took place. On this occasion, also, the male god Dagda and the female goddess, Morrigan, would come together and through their intercourse re-energize the tribe and all of its productiveness. The strong tradition behind this festival survives to the present day as Hallowe'en and its Christianized version, the Feast of All Souls. The next festival, *Imbolc*, observed on February 1, celebrated the end of winter and the return of light. It is also thought to have been associated with the goddess Brigid, a goddess of fertility who, in Christian mythology, became St. Brigid and whose feast day of February 1 is still celebrated widely in Ireland. *Beltane*, celebrated on May 1, was in honor of the Celtic god of fire, Belenus. *Lugnasad*, observed on August 1, was the feast of thanks to the god *Lug* for the harvest bounty. In Gaul this was the occasion when the Gaulish *consilium* met until its venue was relocated to Rome by Emperor Augustus.

CHRISTIANITY REPLACES DRUIDISM

Christianity began encroaching on Gaulish Druidism perhaps as early as the first century. And by the end of the fourth century, when Constantine had converted (312), the church's organization was falling into shape. It is St. Martin, regarded as the true apostle of Gaul, who is given much of the credit for spreading the Gospel to the Gaulish people. He was elected bishop of Tours in 371 A.D., an episcopate he held for twenty-six years. He also founded the monastery of Marmoutier near Tours. The form of Christianity favored by Martin was monastic and to some extent reclusive; this was only natural, as he had come from Bythinia where the monastic form of Christianity was the more prevalent in the Egyptian desert and indeed throughout the east. Although it was completely alien to the Christianity which was gradually establishing itself throughout Gaul, essentially episcopal in character, monasticism took root. Meanwhile, the episcopal form of Christianity spread among the ruling classes in Gaul and was playing an ever-increasing role as civil institutions disintegrated. By the fifth century Druidism was banished. Deprived of its sanctuaries and its druids, it gradually succumbed to Christianity.

Christianity is thought to have come to Britain at the same time, or somewhat later, as it came to Gaul. Tertullian (c. 200 A.D.) writes that the Gospel had already reached some parts of the island not yet under Roman control; and, Origen (c. 240) alludes to the Christian faith as a unifying force among the Britons, although he admits that many of the Britons had not yet heard the Gospel. But there are indications that the British Church was already firmly established in certain areas by the fourth century. Three British bishops attended the Council of Arles in 314 A.D.: the bishop of York, the bishop of London, and the bishop of Colchester. It is generally accepted that Christianity had been introduced into Cornwall by the fifth century, but that Druidism lingered on well into the sixth. In the British kingdom of Strathclyde, conversion is attributed to St. Ninian, who died c. 432 A.D. Despite these references, it is acknowledged that the majority of Britons continued to practice Druidism, and only the upper classes adhered to the Christian faith. This would appear to have been collaborated with the resurgence of native Celtic cults in the latter part of the fourth century.

In the post-Roman period much of eastern Britain became heathen following the arrival of the Anglo-Saxons. It wasn't until the seventh century and the arrival of St. Augustine (604–609), sent to Britain by Pope Gregory, that the Anglo-Saxons finally converted to Christianity. Among the Britons to the west and the north, Christianity had already taken root a century and a half earlier when Irish missionaries began to develop an extraordinary zeal for converting in foreign lands. Northern and western Scotland were evangelized by St. Columba and his monks from Iona. Irish monks studied and taught at the monastery of St. David in Wales; and, it is now generally acknowledged that the Anglo-Saxons owe their conversion, not so much to St. Augustine and his monks, but to Irish missionaries.

Throughout this period the Celtic Church, cut off from easy and normal communication with Rome, embarked on its own path and did not keep pace with the many changes and reforms in ceremonies and practice that had been taking place on the Continent. St. Augustine tried unsuccessfully to reconcile the older form practiced by the Celtic Church with the more up-to-date form which he brought with him from the Continent. The British Celtic people were reluctant to change their time-honored ways, and it was not until the Council of Whitby in 664 A.D. that the fundamental differences were ruled in favor of Rome, thus ending the struggle that had separated the Celtic and Roman Churches for so long. Not only did the outcome of Whitby bring the British Church into conformity with Rome, but ultimately the Churches of Ireland, Scotland, Brittany and Wales followed suit.

IRELAND: THE SPREAD OF CELTIC CHRISTIANITY

Christianity, arriving in the fifth century A.D., was the first major outside influence on Ireland's Celtic culture. The first mission by St. Palladius was less than successful in converting the polytheistic druids and their followers. St. Patrick, arriving in 432 A.D., was more successful in persuading the Irish Celts to embrace the New Faith. While the teachings of the Christian Church had a powerful influence on Gaelic culture, they failed to make any substantial transformation to the framework of Celtic society itself. Instead, these teachings adapted organizationally to fit existing Celtic political institutions. St. Patrick is generally thought to have organized his church in accordance with the Continental model of parishes: assembled into dioceses and presided over by bishops. Within a generation of his death, the Irish began embracing monasticism more fully and the Irish church became organized on very different lines, with monasteries rather than parishes as the key units. The consequence was that abbots generally had more power and influence than bishops.

Theories abound as to how this monastic takeover came about. Paul Johnson, in *A History of Christianity*, suggests that trading links between Ireland and the Loire Valley exposed the Irish to the monastic movement flourishing in Gaul at the time. Other writers believe it all began with the arrival of monks in Ireland, fleeing the vast hordes of vandals spreading throughout Gaul following the collapse of Roman rule. The monks brought with them the rules of monasticism pioneered by St. Martin of Tours. Whatever the reason, by the end of the sixth century monasticism became Ireland's dominant religious form, with several hundred monasteries operating throughout the country. Territorial bishoprics gave way to monastic houses whose members owed allegiance to an institution, the head of which was an abbot. Monasteries were not religious institutions in the restricted sense; they existed and flourished as great centers of learning and culture, opening their doors to scholars of all kinds. They helped transform rural Irish society by providing the country with the closest thing to town-like communities. The larger monasteries, such as Cloonmacnoise and Armagh, supported commercial and administrative networks and were centers of trade and law, as well as learning.

The organization of the Irish Church, and especially of the monasteries, was modeled on that of society in general, which was tribal; tribal customs defined all the rules and activities of the monastery. The head of the monastery was both abbot and chief over the community, except for certain spiritual functions such as ordination, confirmation, etc., which were the domain of a bishop. In his temporal capacity of chief he had jurisdiction over the bishop, but in his spiritual capacity he was under the authority of the bishop. The manner of electing a successor to an abbot strongly paralleled that for the election of chief.[6]

CULTURE AND ENTERPRISE

Culturally speaking, Celtic Ireland was, from the seventh century onward, one of the most advanced societies in Europe. Its monks went abroad and became celebrated for spreading learning throughout Britain and Europe. At home and abroad, their enterprise was extraordinary; their illuminated manuscripts artistic, and their scholarship unequaled. They achieved great missionary success wherever they went, whether it was at Iona, Lindisfarne, Luxeuil, Richenau, or elsewhere throughout Europe. Their esteem as religious pathfinders and scholars became well established during the Dark Ages of Europe. Paul Johnson (1995) writes of the Celtic Irish monks: "They were enormously learned in the scriptures, and wonderfully gifted in the arts. They combined exquisite Latin scholarship with a native cultural tradition which went back to the La Tene civilization of the first century. . . ." At a time when barbarians were descending upon European cities, plundering artifacts and burning books, Irish monks and scribes were painstakingly copying the classics of Latin and Greek literature.

One of the most remarkable expeditions of an Irish monk was that of St. Columbanus, born c. 540. He was a tribal leader who was also head of a family monastery. He was a learned man who studied Latin and Greek and read Virgil, Pliny, Horace, Ovid and the writings of the early Fathers of the Church. St. Columbanus left Ireland for Gaul with a shipload of monks in 575. There he began spreading his own austere brand of monastic Christianity with zealous passion. His was one of the most remarkable missionary expeditions in history. By the time he died in 615, he and his followers had spread Christianity across much of France, Italy and Switzerland and had founded more than forty monasteries.

The contribution of men such as St. Columbanus is fittingly told in Thomas Cahill's, *How the Irish Saved Civilization* (1995): "From the fall of Rome to the rise of Charlemagne—

the 'dark ages'—learning, scholarship, and culture disappeared from the European continent. The great heritage of western civilization—from the Greek and Roman classics to Jewish and Christian works—would have been utterly lost were it not for the holy men and women of unconquered Ireland." But Columbanus' success and that of other Irish monks in Europe over time brought the character of Celtic monasticism to the attention of Church authorities who envisioned it as a threat to the Church's oldest and central institution, the episcopate. It was only a matter of time before Rome stepped in to contain and regulate the Celtic monastic movement that had spread throughout Europe. After the collapse of Emperor Justinian's restored empire in Italy, Pope Gregory adopted the Benedictine[7] rule as the norm for monasticism in the West.

---

[1] P.W. Joyce, *A Social History of Ancient Ireland* (1997)

[2] Ibid.

[3] Ibid.

[4] P.W. Joyce, *Old Celtic Romances* (1907)

[5] P.W. Joyce, *A Social History of Ancient Ireland* (1997) [quoting from Da Derga by Stokes]

[6] Ibid.

[7] Devised by St. Benedict (480–547)

CHAPTER 8

CELTIC ART AND LITERATURE

The Celts, a remarkably artistic people, were considered among the finest metal craftsmen of the ancient world. Barry Cunliffe describes them as much more than just craftsmen, suggesting they carried with them a deep knowledge of mythology and used symbols and combinations that were a form of communication; they were the repository and the performers of ancient skills and beliefs, and as such were looked upon as extraordinary human beings. Most of what we know about the creative talent and technological skills of the Celtic craftsmen is from the countless objects of various kinds uncovered by archaeologists, now preserved in museums throughout Ireland, Britain and the Continent.

The term "Celtic art" is invariably used to mean the art of the La Tene culture (that of central Europe before the Roman conquest), but Celtic art continued and flourished in Britain well into the first century A.D. and in Ireland, unaffected from outside influence, for several centuries later. Celtic art must, therefore, be considered as three separate

Silver cauldron with mythological scenes in relief, 2ND–3RD cent. B.C.

traditions: the continental La Tene art style which flourished
from the fifth century until the conquest of Gaul by the
Romans in the first century B.C.; the insular (British and
Irish) La Tene art style which also flourished from the fifth
century B.C., but continued until the Roman conquest in 43
A.D. (and somewhat later in areas beyond Roman control);
and the Celtic insular art tradition which blossomed in Ireland and to a lesser extent in Britain between the fifth and
twelfth centuries A.D. There is also the art of the Hallstatt
Celts (from the pre-La Tene period) which the experts char-
acterize as more of a simple art form with little evidence of
individual artistic expression.

Above, left: *Limestone head, 3ʳᵈ–2ⁿᵈ cent. B.C.* Right: *Bronze head, 3ʳᵈ cent. B.C.*
Below, left: *Group of limestone "têtes coupées," 3ʳᵈ cent. B.C.* Right: *Limestone torso of a warrior, 3ʳᵈ–2ⁿᵈ cent. B.C.*

CONTINENTAL LA TENE ART

La Tene art gets its name from the site in western Switzerland where the first Celtic artifacts of the pre-Roman period were discovered. It is generally acknowledged that this art form developed in the areas alongside the Saar and the Rhine, where it was imported from the south and the southeast in the first half of the fifth century B.C. and where it later spread throughout Celtic Europe. It drew on three main sources to produce a variety of distinct but related styles: native, mainly that of metal-working, evolved from the Urnfield and Hallstatt cultures; classical from Graeco-Etruscan influence; and oriental imitated from eastern sources.

The earliest examples of Celtic art from this period (acquired from archaeological excavations) show richly decorated ornamental objects which unquestionably reveal the ingenuity and skills of the early Celtic craftsmen and artisans. Artists covered the surfaces of their metal work with elaborate carvings of arches and curving tendrils entwining human and animal masks of multiple dimensions of realism and fantasy. They mastered the art of enameling and the technique of producing quality stained glass; and, they devoted meticulous care to the fashioning of ornate weapons: bronze helmets, shields, swords and chain-link armor. The fashioning combined a variety of techniques: casting combined with engraving, punching, tracing and scorping (grooving the metal with an implement known as a "scorper"). Bronze was the most common metal employed, but gold, silver and iron were on occasion ornamented. Coral and glass were sometimes used to enhance the natural surface of the metal.

Helmet, mid-4ᵀᴴ cent. B.C.; copper, iron, and gold.

Not all of the La Tene art, however, was fashioned in metal; there was also some stone and wood sculpture. Celtic stone sculpturing was not all that common, and the two chief areas where they have been found to date are Provence and Germany. Another striking characteristic of La Tene culture is the elaborate decoration of pottery using motifs common to those of the metalworker. An example is from the region between Moselle and Transdanubia where, from the fifth to the third centuries, the prevalence and distribution of pottery with stamped decoration was widespread.

BRITISH LA TENE ART TRADITION

The British La Tene art tradition is a sphere of Celtic art which continued to evolve and flourish in Britain following the conquest of Celtic Europe by the Romans. It had its beginnings about the middle of the third century B.C. when many Rhineland tribes established themselves in southern Britain alongside the indigenous population, essentially of the Hallstatt culture. The newcomers brought with them a fully-developed La Tene art style from which developed, over time, what is termed the "native British tradition," with its distinctive creations and styles. British craftsmen showed a particular expertise for basket patterns.

Archaeology has furnished many tangible remains from this period which attest to the ingeniousness of the British craftsmen. A bronze helmet found at Waterloo Bridge in London (1868), dating from the late first century B.C., consists of a conical cap made out of decorated sheet bronze from the top of which protrude two fearsome horns. A companion to this impressive object is the huge shield found in the River Thames at Battersea (1857), believed to be from early in the first century A.D. It, too, was made from thin sheets of bronze bound together and originally fastened to a leather or wooden backing. The front is covered with a rich array of ornaments, arranged in elegant symmetry. Many gold torques have been found in Britain including the biggest single find made at Snettisham, Norfolk where, between 1948 and 1950, some fifty-eight whole and fragmented torques were found in an impressive series of caches; and, there were still other finds in 1964 and 1968. Lloyd Laing[1] maintains that the Snettisham caches comprise the richest

114

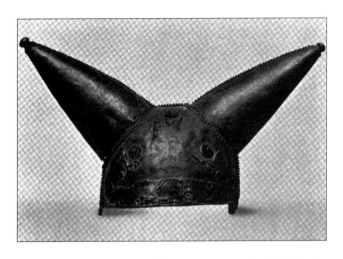

Bronze helmet with conical cap horns, 1ˢᵀ cent. B.C., found at Waterloo Bridge in London.

Bronze ceremonial shield, c. 50 B.C., near Battersea, England.

Above: *Bronze boar, 3ʳᵈ–2ⁿᵈ cent. B.C.*
Below, left: *Bronze horse, incorporated in an object of uncertain use,*
5ᵗʰ cent. B.C.
Below, right: *Bronze helmet, 4ᵗʰ cent. B.C.*

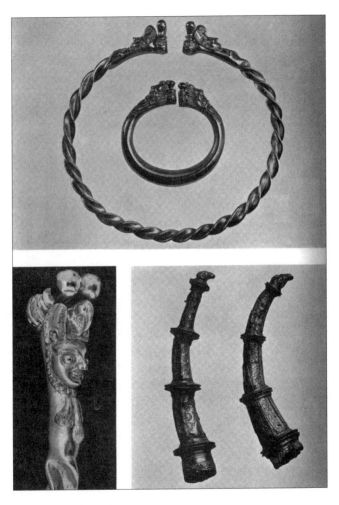

Above: *Gold torque and bracelet, 5ᵀᴴ cent. B.C.* Below, left: *Detail of the torque.* Right: *Small gold horns (possible mounts for oxhorns), second half of 5ᵀᴴ cent. B.C.*

array of Celtic treasures so far excavated from British soil. When compared to the scantiness of other Iron Age finds from East Anglia, they reveal the great contrast in wealth between the nobility and the tribesmen in general.

Except for the Picts and the Scots, little Celtic art of distinction seems to have been produced in Britain after the seventh century A.D. By the thirteenth century, it had disappeared altogether. Although elements of a Celtic tradition have been detected from time to time thereafter, it was not until the conscious revival of Celtic art in the nineteenth century that it became popular again.

IRISH CELTIC ART TRADITION

The third tradition of Celtic art, developed in Ireland between the fifth and twelfth centuries A.D., flourished in four separate fields: ornamentation and illumination of manuscripts, metal-work, stone-carving and to a lesser degree, leatherwork. As in Britain, it had its beginnings in La Tene art which arrived from the Continent about 300 B.C. (superimposing on the earlier Bronze Age tradition) and from which there evolved a tradition that can be traced to its golden era in the early Christian period, its temporary decline with the Viking invasions, and its remarkable renaissance in the eleventh and twelfth centuries.

Throughout its history, the Irish art tradition was closely akin to the European tradition; and, although the foreign sources from which it drew its inspiration varied from one period to another, it was sufficiently vigorous to mold new styles and new ideas into something characteristically and unmistakably Irish.

The ancient Irish Celtic craftsmen and artisans practiced from time immemorial the art of working with bronze, silver, gold and enamel and had become highly proficient with their skills by the time St. Patrick arrived in the fifth century. In the ancient tales and legends, gold and silver ornaments are everywhere mentioned as worn by the upper classes, and these accounts are fully corroborated by the great numbers of objects of both metals that have been found from time to time in various parts of Ireland. Joyce[2] relates how the monarch Tigernmas (*c.* 939 B.C.) first smelted gold in Ireland and first introduced ornaments of gold and silver; how another king, Muinemon, first caused necklets of gold to be worn around the necks of kings and chiefs; and how a third king, Fail-derg-doid, was the first to cause rings of gold to be worn on the fingers of chiefs in Ireland.

However true these ancient tales are, the fact remains that there is a great collection of ancient ornamental objects, some of pure gold, some of silver and some of mixed metals and precious stones, now preserved in the National Museum of Ireland in Dublin. Those from the Christian era are decorated with the peculiar patterns known as *opus Hibernicum*: "interlaced work formed by bands, ribbons and cords which are curved and twisted and interwoven in the most intricate way, something like basketwork infinitely varied in pattern." Those of the pre-Christian era have no interlaced work, but only spirals, circles, zigzags, parallel lines, etc. Among the articles which have been recovered (and are on display in the National Museum) are three of extraordinary craftsmanship

119

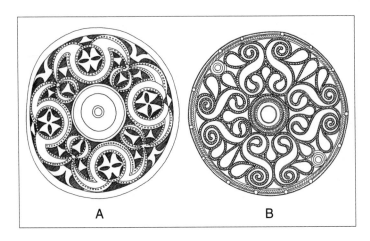

Celtic decorative motifs. (a) *Bronze roll-rim;* (b) *Gold appliqué disk. 5ᵀᴴ–4ᵀᴴ cent. B.C.*

and astonishing beauty: the Ardagh Chalice, the Tara Brooch and the Cross of Cong.

The Ardagh Chalice, standing seven inches high and more than nine inches in diameter at its top, is elaborately ornamented with designs in metal and enamel. It was found in more recent times buried under a large rock at Ardagh, County Limerick and is believed to have been crafted sometime before the tenth century. Margaret Stokes[3] describes it as combining "classic beauty of form with the most exquisite examples of almost every variety of Celtic ornamentation. . . ." She further states that its decorative designs, of which there are about forty different varieties, all show "a freedom of inventive power and play of fancy only equalled by the work upon the so-called Tara Brooch."

Ardagh Chalice, County Limerick.

Tara Brooch, underside.

The Tara Brooch—extensively ornamented with amber, glass, enamel, and distinctive Irish filigree (interlaced work in metal)—and its extraordinary delicacy and beauty make it, perhaps, the finest example of Celtic craftsmanship found anywhere. Found in 1850 near Drogheda, its crafting is thought to be contemporaneous with that of the Ardagh Chalice. There are many other handsome brooches, such as the Ardagh Brooch, the Roscrea Brooch, the Dal Riada Brooch, etc.—each with a particular beauty of its own. But, for beauty, none of them equals the Tara Brooch. Both the face of the brooch and the back are overlaid with seventy-six different kinds of beautiful patterns, each designed in such diminutive precision that its perfection of detail can easily escape the naked eye.

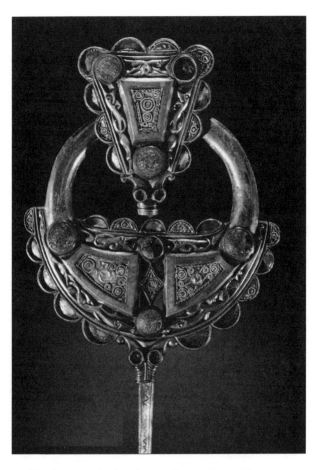

Pseudopenannular brooch, near Roscrea, County Tipperary.

The Cross of Cong, thirty inches in height, was a processional cross made to enshrine a piece of the true cross. Its surface is done over with painstaking adornment of clear Celtic design. A sequence of inscriptions in Gaelic describe how it was made in 1123 by order of Turlogh O'Conor, king of Connacht, for the church in Tuam then administered by Archbishop Muredach O'Duffy; the inscription also names the artist as Mailisa Mac Braddan O'Hechan.

Some of the finest metalwork is exhibited on shrines, called *cumdachs*, made to protect the valuable manuscripts of the time. These book-shrines were mostly made from the eighth century to the twelfth; some of the finest are those of the *Book of Kells*, the *Book of Durrow* and the *Book of Armagh*, and several are preserved in the National Museum, Dublin. There were also belt-shrines, such as the one from Moylourg consisting of leather strips richly ornamented with metal-work, used to enclose relics. Other types were the crozier-shrine used to cover the *bachall*, and the bell-shrine to enclose a bell.

Artistic stone-carving (which developed quite apart from that of metal-work, although the motifs are often interchangeable) is chiefly exhibited in the great stone crosses—more than fifty of which are still standing in many parts of Ireland. Besides the elaborate ornamentation, most of the crosses display groups of figures representing various matters of religious history intended to impress upon those who were illiterate the messages of scripture and religious history by vivid illustration. One feature of the Irish Celtic cross is the circular ring which, according to Joyce, was developed in Ireland. A few high crosses of the Irish type are found in southern Scotland and northern England, but it is acknowledged that they were crafted by Irish artists or under their influence.

Processional Cross of Cong.

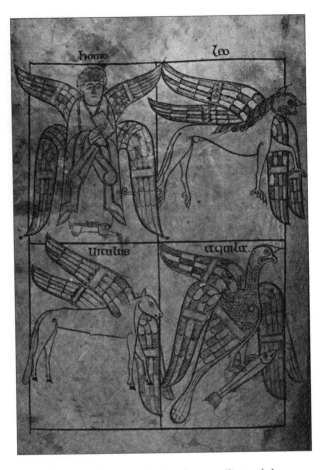

The Book of Armagh, fol. *32v: the evangelist symbols.*

"Corp Naomh" bell-shrine, Templecross, County Westmeath.

West face of Muiredach's cross, about A.D. 922, Monasterboice, County Louth. Bottom: *the arrest of Christ.*

THE ILLUMINATED MANUSCRIPT

Ireland's crowning artistic achievement was the creation of a new medium: illuminating manuscripts with a special style of pen adornment. This finely-wrought artistry on parchment was the product of successive generations of artists who brought it to astonishing perfection using Coptic motifs along with patterns from Celtic and Anglo-Saxon metalwork, (pagan and Christian) to mold a characteristically Irish Celtic art. It was chiefly the work of monks and it is believed to have started at Columbanus' monastery at Bobbio, whose Irish monks had continuing contact with the homeland as well as with the East.[4] Many of these manuscripts have survived, among them masterpieces such as the *Book of Durrow*, the *Lindisfarne Gospels*, and the *Book of Kells*.

The first of the surviving manuscripts with illustrations is the *Book of Durrow*, penned sometime between 670–680 A.D. and named for one of St. Columba's earliest and most important monasteries in Ireland. It has elaborate "carpet" pages devoted to nothing but decoration in a style that is "anticlassical, abstract and symbolic, unlike anything found in Continental medieval manuscripts."[5] Stunningly intricate as it is, the *Book of Durrow*, being one of the earliest of the illuminated manuscripts, is said to lack the skill and scope manifest of later works. The *Lindisfarne Gospels*, penned in the eighth century, is another jewel. Its carpet pages are similar to those of the *Book of Durrow* but, according to the examiners, are more meticulously drawn: "clear and delicate, like finely-woven tapestries." The Lindisfarne manuscript was Irish in origin, but the work was mostly done by Irish-trained English clerics.

The Book of Durrow, fol. *191v: the lion, symbol of St. Mark.*

The Lindisfarne Gospels, fol. *210R, late 7^m century.*

The Book of Kells, fol. *7v: the Virgin and Child with angels.*

The *Book of Kells*, a vellum manuscript in Latin, is regarded as the greatest and most beautiful of the Gospel manuscripts. Its precise origin is unknown but, according to some experts, it was penned in Kells, County Meath; yet others attribute the work to the Irish monks at St. Columba's monastery in Iona (Scotland). Its exact age is also unknown, but most agree that it was probably written in the seventh or early eighth century. Rich in imagery, beautiful in design and color, and laden with allusion and symbolism, the *Book of Kells* is nothing short of Celtic craftsmanship at its highest perfection. It is the last great manuscript of Ireland's golden age. The ninth and tenth centuries saw nothing of this dimension: many of the great illuminators were killed in the Viking raids or escaped to the Continent. In the eleventh and twelfth centuries there were some interesting creations, but these later works are said to not have approached the brilliance and intricacy of the earlier masterpieces.

Following the Anglo-Norman invasion of Ireland at the end of the twelfth century, the Irish artistic tradition began a gradual decline into a twilight zone where it reposed until the early nineteenth century. It then became popular again, fueled by nationalistic inspiration and a reawakening to the richness of the Celtic tradition.

[1] Lloyd Laing, *Celtic Britain* (1979)

[2] P.W. Joyce, *A Social History of Ancient Ireland* (1997)

[3] Seumas MacManus, *The Story of the Irish Race* (1972)

[4] Katherine Scherman, *The Flowering of Ireland* (1981)

[5] Ibid. [author's analysis based upon Harry Bober's, "Celtic Christian Art: Form and Meaning," lectures presented at New York's Metropolitan Museum of Art, fall 1977]

CHAPTER 9

IRELAND'S HEROIC AGE

Ireland's popular epics have bequeathed to posterity a vivacious and exciting portrayal of the ancient Celts, opening a window to a world astonishingly similar to that which Diodorus, Strabo, Caesar and others encountered in Gaul before the Roman conquest. Through these epics we have an understanding of Ireland's Heroic Age (climaxing shortly before the arrival of Christianity) when kings fought kings and warriors stole wives, and where the rustling of cattle was a recurrent pretense for going to war. As in old Gaul, the brave men of Ireland's sagas dressed in woolen cloaks pinned together at the neck by a brooch. Trousers were worn only by the poor, noblemen preferring *leine*, a knee-length linen tunic. The weaponry of a warrior consisted of two or three javelins or the long lance and sword which, as in the La Tene period, was suitable for "cutting but not for thrusting." Bows and arrows seem to have been known to the early Irish as to the Gauls before Caesar's day.[1]

The Celtic Ireland of the Heroic Age was a society of Iron Age aristocrats and warriors with a culture very much akin to that of Homeric Greece. The romantic stories of this era are presented in vivid and lavish detail in a series of sagas handed down orally by many generations of poets and storytellers, and later put into writing by monks. Most of the legends fall under three cycles: the Cycle of Conchobar mac Nessa of Ulster and his Red Branch Knights who existed in the first century A.D.; the Cycle of the Fena of Erin belonging to a period two centuries later; and, legends founded on events that happened after the dispersal of the Fena (at the end of the third century).

The stories of Conchobar and the Red Branch Knights form the finest part of Ireland's ancient romantic literature. The most celebrated tale is the *Tain Bo Cuailnge* relating to the long, drawn-out struggle waged between the men of Ulster and the men of Connacht. This tale describes feats, passion and battles between the great warriors of the court of Conchobar at Emain Macha and those of the court of Meave at Rathcroghan in present-day County Roscommon.

THE STORY OF THE *TAIN BO CUAILNGE*

The *Tain Bo Cuailnge*, or the Cattle Raid of Cooley, is a marvelous epic about a classic encounter between two self-important monarchs: Conchobar who, as king of Ulster, reigned from his stronghold at Emain, and Meave, the combative queen of Connacht who resided with her consort, Ailill, at Rathcroghan. In the prelude to the epic there is the legend of the beautiful young Deirdre whom the old king,

Conchobar, insists on marrying. Instead, she falls in love with Naisi and elopes with him to Alba. Conchobar, although infuriated at their elopement, pretends to forgive them and sends his trusted servant Fergus mac Roth to Alba to entice them to return to Ireland. Conchobar, however, goes back on his word and has Deirdre's husband Naisi and his two brothers (described as the sons of Usnach) who have eloped with them, put to death. Fergus and his followers, enraged with Conchobar for breaking his word, defect to Queen Meave, Conchobar's chief enemy. Meanwhile, Deirdre flings herself from a fast-moving chariot to her death.

Next, the story relates the rivalry between Meave and her consort, Ailill, as to their respective possessions. This leads to Meave's ensuing expedition into Ulster at the head of a great army of Connachtmen to harass her former husband, King Conchobar, and to confiscate the Brown Bull of Cooley. In the opening scenario, Meave and her husband, Ailill, each boast of having riches and livestock greater than the other. When they are finished counting and comparing their herds, Meave becomes furious at discovering that Ailill has a gorgeous white bull among his herd which she cannot match.

She immediately sends her envoys to every corner of Ireland to find a bull that will match Ailill's. After an intensive search, they find such a bull in the herd of Daire mac Fiachniu of Cuailnge in Ulster, popularly referred to as the Bull of Cuailnge. It is so huge "that a hundred warriors could find shade from the heat in its shadow," and it is remarkably virile in that "every day it would bestride fifty cows, which calved the very next day." An exhilarated Meave immediately orders her envoys to procure him; however, their arrogance and boastfulness during a banquet at mac Fiachniu's

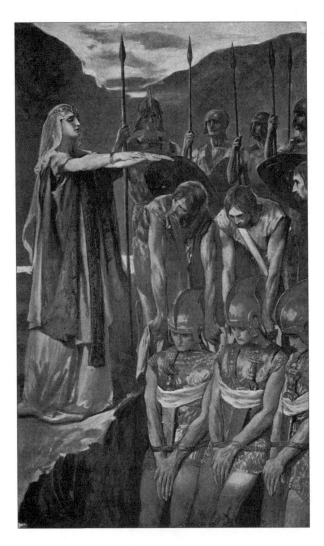

Deirdre's lament.

Queen Meave's cairn, Knocknarea, Sligo.

house results in a breakdown in the negotiations, and they must return to Connacht without the bull.

Furious, Meave mobilizes a great army of *Fir Domnainn* knights (Connacht's equivalent of Ulster's Red Branch Knights) under their leader Ferdiad, allied forces from other parts of Ireland, and the defectors from Ulster under Fergus (eager to strike at Conchobar for having killed their brave comrades, the three sons of Usnach). They march on Ulster to do battle with Conchobar and his Red Branch fighting men, led by the gallant Cuchullian. Throughout the story, Cuchullian is shown to embody the archetype of the Celtic warrior-aristocrat, possessing courage, honor, unmatched haughtiness and a nonchalance for death; he is henceforth the hero and the great central figure of the *Tain*. There is also Cuchullian the demigod who, in preparation for battle, transforms into a figure with the hideous malformation of one of the Celtic gods:

> His body made a furious twist inside his skin, so that his feet and shins switched to the rear and his heels and calves switched to the front . . . On his head the temple-sinews stretched to the nape of his neck, each mighty, immense, measureless knob as big as the head of a month-old child . . . He sucked one eye so deep into his head that a wild crane couldn't probe it onto his cheek out of the depths of his skull; the other eye fell out along his cheek . . . His cheek peeled back from his jaws until the gullet appeared, his lungs and liver flapped in

his mouth and throat . . . The hair of his head twisted like the tangle of a red thornbush . . . If a royal apple tree with all its kingly fruit were shaken above him, scarce an apple would reach the ground but each would be spiked on a bristle of his hair as it stood up on his scalp with rage . . . Then, tall and thick, steady and strong, high as the mast of a noble ship, rose up from the dead centre of his skull a straight spout of black blood darkly smoking.[2]

A detailed account of the battle follows, describing how Cuchullian single-handedly fights Meave's army: "One by one the great warriors of Connacht were sent against him and one by one he fells them." Meave, infuriated at the number of her men he is slaying, sends one hundred warriors against him all at once. He slews them "two and three at a time day and night and for three months he knew no rest except for short naps whenever he could." Champion after champion battle and are overcome by Cuchullian, until finally he has to battle with his foster-brother, Ferdiad. Meave has offered her daughter, Finnabair, in marriage to Ferdiad if he would fight his old friend. From O'Curry's translation of the *Tain*, we have the following description of the hand-to-hand fighting between Cuchullian and Ferdiad:

Each of them began to cast spears at the other, from the full middle of the day till the close of the evening; and though the warding off was of the best, still the throwing was so superior, that each of them bled, reddened and wounded the other, in that time. 'Let us desist from this, now O Cuchullian,' said Ferdiad. 'Let us desist,' said Cuchullian.

They ceased. They threw away their arms from them into the hands of their charioteers. Each of them approached the other forthwith, and each put his hands around the other's neck, and gave him three kisses. Their horses were in the same paddock that night, and their charioteers at the same fire; and their charioteers spread beds of green rushes for them, fitted with wounded men's pillows. The professors of healing and curing came to heal and cure them, and they applied herbs and plants of healing and curing to their stabs and their cuts and their gashes and to all their wounds. Of every herb and of every healing and curing plant that was put to the stabs and cuts and gashes and to all the wounds of Cuchullian, he would send an equal portion from him westward over the ford to Ferdiad, so that the men of Eirinn might not be able to say, should Ferdiad fall by him, that it was by better means of cure that he was enabled (to kill him).

Of each kind of food, and of palatable, pleasant, intoxicating drink that was sent by the men of Eirinn to Ferdiad he would send a fair moiety over the ford northwards to Cuchullian because the purveyors of Ferdiad were more numerous than the purveyors of Cuchullian.

On the evening of the second day following another fierce encounter:

They threw their arms from them into the hands of their charioteers. Each of them came towards the other. Each of them put his hands round the neck of the other, and bestowed three kisses on him. Their horses were in the same enclosure, and their charioteers at the same fire.

For several days the two warriors fight more fiercely, more terribly than ever until Ferdiad finally manages to thrust his sword into Cuchullian's shoulder. It is then that Cuchullian calls on Laegh for his most famous weapon, the *Gae Bulga*, or belly spear, and with it he finally brings down Ferdiad. "The end has come at last, O Cuchullian," Ferdiad whispers, and he drops to the ground.

We are reminded of the striking parallelism between the fight of Cuchullian and Ferdiad and that in the Greek epic between Achilles and Hector. As in the fight between Achilles and Hector, there is something inequitable about this contest: like Achilles, Cuchullian is shown to be semi-divine, and as Achilles has divine protective covering, so does Cuchullian possess a secret weapon which he ultimately uses to kill Ferdiad.

The young Ulster warrior fights valiantly, just as he had in the many other sagas describing his feats. Again and again we encounter him in the traditional affrays defending his hero's role. On one occasion while walking with his sweetheart, Emer, he is confronted by an unusually brash youth challenging him to a fight. Although he has been warned by Emer that the boy is in fact his son, Cuchullian takes up the challenge, for he "would not let a child call into question the honour of the men of Ulster." After striking the fatal blow, he

Cuchullian carries Ferdiad.

Cuchullian is warned by Emer.

145

picks up the limp body in his arms and carries it back to the camp where the men of Ulster are gathered. "This is my son," he tells them, and from that time he is seen by his friends to have become greatly despondent.

But, noble as Cuchullian was, he was destined to die young. Of the several myths surrounding his death there is the one where Meave is reputed to have used her magical powers to enfeeble him in battle against Erc—the battle that resulted in his death. Knowing that he is dying, Cuchullian ties himself to a column so that he may die erect and honorably, having the war-goddess *Badh* in the form of a raven perched upon his shoulder.

THE CYCLE OF FINN AND THE FENA

The heroic stories in the Cycle of Finn and the Fena, preserved in a collection of poems by Oisin (the chief bard of the Fena) under the title of *Agallam na Seanorach* (the Colloquy of the Ancients), relate to a warrior class lasting for most of a century from the reign of Conn (177–212 A.D.) to that of Carbery (279–297). The Fena attained their greatest power during the reign of Cormac mac Art (254–277), under their most celebrated leader, Finn MacCool. Admittance into the Fena was very exclusive, and only candidates who had demonstrated extraordinary strength and bravery were picked. The entrant had to sever all ties with family and home, and undergo rigorous training in combat and athletic feats. The physical ordeals of initiation were harsh: each candidate was required to stand in a waist-high trench armed only with his shield and a short hazel branch. With these, he had to ward off the spears thrown by the warriors; and, if one touched him he was thereupon disqualified. He had to braid his hair and run through the forest pursued by others. He could not be wounded or captured, his weapon could not tremble in his hand, nor a twig crack under his foot, nor a branch disturb one braid of his hair. He had to be able to draw a thorn out of his foot while running, leap over a stick as high as his forehead, and streak under one level with his knee.

When accepted, he was, with his companions, in the unusual position of being outside society but not outside the law. In the summertime, they roamed the forests and led a life of the foot-loose hunter-warrior; during the wintertime, they lived off the people, keeping their foraging to a minimum. Though they lived by hunting, plundering and warfare, they were not considered bandits. Each was sworn to fight to protect the high-king, to keep peace among the subkings and petty chiefs, and to guard the country against foreign attack (conceivably, they were concerned about a Roman invasion from neighboring Britain). While committed to defend and safeguard the high-king, their oath of loyalty was not to him but to their leader, Finn MacCool.

Finn was the chief hero of the Fena, and under him were his son, Oisin and his grandson, Oscar. There were other characters who provided vitality and coherence throughout the tales, among them Goll Mac Morna leader of the Connacht Fena, Cailte Mac Ronan the swift-footed, and Conan the Bald, described as foul-mouthed, boastful, cowardly and gluttonous. While the main characters in the tales are chiefly historical, some of the tales are embellished with fiction; others are regarded as altogether fictitious, or as Joyce describes them, "pure creations of the imagination."

Over the course of time the Fena became powerful and arrogant. Though ascetic in their ideals, they did not abstain from women: they had first right to the girls of the tribe who could not be given in marriage before they were offered to the Fena. This occasionally made the Fena unpopular, and it eventually led to their downfall. It happened when the elderly Finn fell in love with Cormac's beautiful daughter, Grania. Grania would have no part of Finn and she arranged to elope with another member, the youthful Dermott.

After this episode there arose dissension in the Fena; Finn had shown himself ready to put his affection for Grania above the interests of the organization. There were other problems as well; the Fena were becoming too pretentious, and there were demands that their activities needed restraining. It was Cormac's son, Carbery, who eventually brought them to their knees at the battle of Gowra in 280 A.D. Oisin, Finn's son, led the Fena against Carbery's forces in one of the fiercest fights of ancient times. Oisin's son, Oscar, was killed, as were most of the Fena warriors. After the defeat, Oisin vanished to Tir na nOg (the Land of Eternal Youth); it is on his sojourn there and his return to Ireland, that the tale proceeds. Oisin returns to an Ireland in which the Fena are long forgotten. He meets St. Patrick and relates to him the heroic tales of the past. From this point on, Ireland emerges from myth and legend into the world of real history.

In the Irish sagas, we find that women play important and sometimes predominant roles. They are always ladies; for instance, Meave in the story of the Cooley bull: "Although

148

King Ailill was the ruler, his queen always had the final word in the land of Connacht, for she could order whatever she liked, take as lover whomsoever she desired, and could get rid of them as she felt inclined. She was strong and restless, like a goddess of war, and she knew no law other than her strong will. She was, it was said, tall with a long, pallid countenance and she had hair the colour of ripe corn. When Fergan [the adventurer] came to see her in her palace at Roscommon, she gave him her love as to many others before."

ARTHURIAN TALES

The latest cycle of Celtic mythical tales is that of King Arthur and the Knights of the Round Table which recount events of that period in Britain commonly referred to as the Dark Age. The actual literary starting point for the tales connected with the Round Table was when Nennius, a ninth century monk, in his *Historia Britonnum* (History of the Britons), wrote that "Arthur fought together with the other British kings against the Saxons, and was their commander-in-chief."[3] Nennius also describes how the Celts fought in twelve battles with the Germanic invaders, the last of them on Mount Badon, on which "there fell in one day nine hundred and forty men. Arthur killed them at the first attempt. No one other than Arthur was capable of defeating these enemies. He was the victor in all the action."

Whether the real Arthur ever existed may not be that significant, for it is the legendary Arthur who has illuminated the history of Britain's "dark centuries" after the withdrawal of the Romans. Following the departure of Roman rule in the

King Arthur's Castle, Tintagel.

fifth century, Saxon tribes pushed the native Britons further back and further out of their communities. Many took refuge in Wales, where they re-established themselves among their western kinfolk; others fled to Cornwall or to Gaul. As the annalists tell it, they took with them the memories of their hopeless struggle and tragic downfall not only in their songs and ballads, but also in the myths that safeguarded, for them, the essence of the Celtic soul from worldly influences. It suited the Celts' style, for they were people who never came to terms with reality; if conditions became intolerable, they invariably found sanctuary in their imagination—the most successful of which was the creation of the kingdom ruled by King Arthur.

Many historians believe that King Arthur was probably the historical figure Vortigern who took over in eastern Britain around 425 after the last Roman left, and whose court was served by the magician Merlin (also a chief figure of Arthurian legend). It was Merlin who forewarned doom for the Britons in the battle of the two mythical dragons—one symbolizing the Celts, the other symbolizing the Saxons. According to the Arthurian tales, Vortigern is defeated and killed by two Celtic chieftains who have returned from Brittany. One of them has the name of the presumed last Roman commander in Britain, Ambrosius Aurelius; the other, his brother, is called Uther Pendragon. Ambrosius, in many of the versions, is Merlin's father, which makes Uther his uncle. Both rule in succession over the territory they have captured from Vortigern, and they retain the young magician, Merlin, as their closest advisor. Later, Arthur arrives on the scene, the offspring of an involuntary illicit affair of the beautiful Igerna, wife of Duke Gorlois of Cornwall, and Uther who

151

The magician Merlin.

seduced her after Merlin had transformed him into her husband's appearance. The youth born from this union later appears before a group of Celtic noblemen in London; they are exploring what they should do with a stone they have come across, into which a sword has been imbedded bearing the inscription that he who would extract it should become king of Britain. Hitherto, no one had managed the feat of extracting the sword; now, it is Arthur's turn. Without any effort, he pulls out the sword, thus becoming the first in line to the kingship upon Uther's death.

Arthur becomes king and Britain enters the heroic epoch. He selects Camelot (a place no one has yet identified) as his residence and marries Guinevra, daughter of the dwarf-king Leodegrance. He selects one hundred and fifty knights (the number that can be seated at his huge round table) with swords vastly superior to those in the hands of all mortal foes. Arthur defeats the Picts, Saxons and Scots and, when summoned by the Roman emperor to pay tribute, he heads to the Continent where he forces the Roman legions back to the Tiber. Returning from this campaign, he does battle with rebellious British chiefs and from time to time embarks on unusual adventures. His fairy-tale biography fills in a century of British history in such a way that historians have yet to discern where it overlaps with factual history.

The saga of Arthur was further complicated in the early twelfth century when the Normans, comparative newcomers to England, wished to establish hereditary ties on the island. One thing they were not was Anglo-Saxon, and therefore claims to a Saxon progenitor was not in their interest. On the other hand, similarities between the Normans and the Celtic Britons were more appealing, probably because many of the knights who arrived and had fought with William were descendants of British Celts. A suitable hero had to be found, and Arthur fit the role. Like the Normans he had fought the Saxons, and again like the Normans he was the victor. It was about then that the story of Arthur was resurrected by the librarian of Malmesbury. Through him, word of Arthur reached the Earl of Gloucester after which Geoffrey of Monmouth included him in his *History of the Kings of Britain*. Almost overnight Geoffrey's fiction became England's fact. Henry II named his grandson Arthur (1187) in the hope that he would one day become Arthur II of England. The Welsh were outraged that their hero should suddenly be adopted by the Norman English.

While the Arthurian cycle can be interpreted to fit many different viewpoints, Jean Markale (1978) makes the point that the Saxon invasions were, in a sense, the last straw for the Britons whose Celtic society was already severely weakened by Roman subjugation; that is, the bitter taste of defeat gave them a natural longing for revenge, but since they were materially too weak to retaliate and since the ancient Celtic world was crumbling away, vengeance gave way to myth-making. It was through this myth-making that the Britons ultimately achieved their finest victory, turning every defeat into a magical adventure where the erosion of Celtic society could be attributed to supernatural events. In this way, says Markale, the myth of the supreme king or leader came into being, and with it came Arthur who reigned not only over Wales where his legend was first born, but also over the kingdoms of Logres and Lloegr,[4] over Brittany and Gaul, and even over Rome.

[1] Gerhard Herm, *The Celts* (1977)

[2] Katherine Scherman, *The Flowering of Ireland* (1981) [source for the *Tain* references]

[3] Gerhard Herm, *The Celts* (1977)

[4] That is the whole of Britain excluding Scotland

CHAPTER 10

THE INSULAR CELTS: THE LAST BULWARK

Throughout the early Middle Ages, several Celtic communities survived in different stages of isolation on the western fringes of Europe: in Wales, Cornwall, Ireland, Scotland and Brittany. Wales and the Highlands of Scotland remained Celtic and unconquered until the arrival of the Normans. Together with the neighboring island of Ireland, they formed the last bulwark of what remained of the Celtic civilization which had dominated Europe before the rise of the Roman Empire.

Most of eastern and southeastern Britain had come under Saxon jurisdiction by the sixth century. According to legend, it was the battle of Camlann (541 A.D.), in which King Arthur was killed, that was the decisive element for Anglo-Saxon dominance. After this defeat there followed a period of upheaval and turmoil when various British leaders attempted to organize anti-Saxon resistance; but, they were unsuccessful because of constant feuding and incessant hostilities among the leaders. Then more fragmented than ever, Britons reluctantly relinquished their territories to the ever-expanding Angles and Saxons. Only three areas survived, the largest of which was Wales. A second area included Cornwall and part of Devon in the southwest. The third, the kingdom of Cumbria, lay to the north on the Pictish border.

For the next century or two the Britons of Cumbria engaged in fierce fighting on two fronts: against the Saxons on their southern border and against the Picts to the north. In 750 A.D. they fought a fierce battle against the Picts at Mocetwawc in which the Pictish king Talargan, son of Fergus, and the British leader, Tewdur, were both killed. Ten years later these same northern Britons fought the Saxons at the battle of Hereford where Tewdur's son, Dyvnwal, was killed. In 784 and 788 Offa, king of Mercia, wreaked havoc on the Cumbria Britons. He was challenged in 795 A.D. by Meredydd, king of the Demetae, at the battle of Rhuddlan; but, the British leader was killed and the northern Britons surrendered.

WALES

The strength of Welsh resistance to the Saxons was quite remarkable despite the fact that they had to deal as well with Irish invaders on their coastal border. In 822 the Saxons destroyed the fortress of Deganwy near Conway and tried to occupy the central Welsh kingdom of Powys. King Cynnen held out against them for many years but was finally taken prisoner in 850 and is said to have died in Rome in 854. Moreover, a new foe had appeared on the horizon: Norsemen attacked and devastated the island of Mona in 858. In 877,

Rhodri Mawr (the Great), who was then king of Wales, was killed in battle and the kingship of Wales was divided between his sons: Cadell receiving Cardigan, Anarawt receiving Gwynedd and Mervyn winning Powys. The annalists describe how Cadell seized Powys from Mervyn (876), who was later killed by his own vassals. Meanwhile, Anarawt was fighting the Saxons, winning a significant victory from them at Conway in 880. He joined forces with the Angles in 894 to ravage Cardigan and other settlements. When his brother Cadell died in 909, he became king of all Wales. Anarawt died in 915.

Throughout this period the Vikings continued to attack both Saxons and Britons alike. Periodically, the belligerents would put aside their differences so they could join forces in a united front against the Vikings. However, such alliances were temporary, and Welsh resistance to the Saxons continued into the reign of Howel Dda (the son of Cadell) who ruled Wales from 915 to 950. Howel was one of the last kings who succeeded in unifying the Welsh kingdoms under a single monarchy. In 937, he set out to reunite all Britons— Welshmen, Cornishmen, Cumbrians, and even Irishmen, Picts and Danes—into a coalition to drive out the Saxons, but was unsuccessful. After his death, the Welsh began to fight again amongst themselves, and their feuding, lasting into the eleventh century, weakened their resolve to continue. Llywelyn ab Gruffyd (1246–1282), the last of the Welsh kings, spent his life trying to protect Welsh sovereignty. Under his leadership Wales had become a strong Celtic kingdom for a while. However, the Normans were pushing into Wales and, in 1277, they demanded he surrender all claims to homage from the other Welsh chiefs. He died fighting the Normans at Buelt in 1282, and Wales, which had for centuries successfully defended itself against the Saxons, was now compelled to surrender its sovereignty to the Normans. The conflict, however, was a comparatively peaceful one as the Welsh had much in common with the Normans. Many of the soldiers who had accompanied William the Conqueror were Breton Celts (descendants of Britons who escaped to Brittany when the Saxons arrived), eager to avenge the Saxon conquest of their ancestral homeland.

Wales was incorporated under the English Crown pursuant to the *Statute of Rhuddlan* in 1284; the kingdom was divided into shires with English courts and law replacing the existing system. Edward I of England (1272–1307), accorded the title Prince of Wales to his son, the future Edward II. While Welsh political independence ended in 1284, complete union with England did not come until 1536. In the meantime, there was an unsuccessful attempt to again unite Wales under native leadership. By 1536, however, Celtic Wales was completely under English domination, except for their language, customs and rich Celtic culture which they tenaciously guarded throughout the centuries.

SCOTLAND

Scotland was a very divided kingdom in early times, inhabited by four peoples with four languages: Picts, the oldest inhabitants, in the northeast; Britons (akin to Welsh) south of the Antonine Wall; Scots (Irish) in the northwest; and Angles, the newest arrivals, who spread gradually westward superimposing an Anglian overlordship on the native population between the Forth and the Tyne. An invasion from Ireland in the fifth century completely changed the history of Scotland north of the Highland line, as Scotti colonists (as the Irish were then called) imposed their Gaelic (Q-Celtic) language and eventually extended their political sway over the native Picts of the region.

At the time of the Norman Conquest, Scotland consisted of two main regions: the northern half beyond the "Highland line" which was purely Celtic and where Celtic tribal customs continued to hold sway; and the southern half with its solid Anglo-Saxon influence, and from where there appeared to have been some acknowledgment of subservience to the English Crown before the Normans arrived. After the Conquest, Norman barons moved into the area and established a firm feudal system which empowered Anglo-Norman kings, Henry II in particular, to demand homage from fiefs in the area.

In the thirteenth century Edward I, fresh from his conquest of Wales, made the first move to consolidate Scotland under the jurisdiction of the English Crown. His opportunity came in 1290 when the reigning Scottish king, who had met a tragic death, left the heirship to a three-year-old Norwegian granddaughter, the child of his daughter (who had died at the infant's birth) and of the king of Norway. Edward, fearing that Scotland might be absorbed into the kingdom of Norway, mediated with the Scots and the king of Norway to have the infant queen contracted in marriage to his son, the slightly younger Prince of Wales. Unfortunately, this peaceful union of the two realms was not to be realized for another three hundred years—all because the little "Maid of Norway," a delicate child, died before her marriage to the prince could come about, thus leaving behind a divided nation and an unclear succession.

Edward immediately stepped into the fray, declaring himself overlord of Scotland until the rightful heir was chosen. His haughtiness in dealing with the northern kingdom, however, aroused deep resentment among the Scottish people. Furthermore, his demand that Scotland furnish troops for English wars pushed the Scots into an alliance with the French, Edward's enemies at the time. Edward wasted little time in suppressing the dissident Scots. He led an army into Scotland, captured Edinburgh, defeated the rebels at the battle of Dunbar and took over the administration of the kingdom, appointing Englishmen to administer in his absence. Adding insult to injury, he confiscated their historic Stone of Scone, which had long been used in the coronation of Scottish kings, and carried it back to Westminster. Within a year after Edward's invasion the Scots rebelled again, rallying behind a guerrilla leader named William Wallace who inflicted a spectacular defeat on an English force at Stirling Bridge, a gateway into the Highlands. The following year, Edward hurried back from his French campaign and led a successful campaign into Scotland, putting an end to the sovereignty move and Wallace's brief ascendancy.

Finally in 1603 (during the reign of James I), Scotland joined England under the same Crown while keeping her own parliament for the time being. A half century later Cromwell forced a union of the two kingdoms and, in 1707, Scotland gave up her separate parliament and nominal independence and entered into a complete union with England. But the Act of Union primarily involved the Lowlands. Beyond the Highland line was another Scotland where the clansmen cared little for the authority of English law or king; to them, the paternalistic chief was everything. They preserved more of their Celtic heritage, holding onto their language and customs. Mostly Catholic and poor, they had little contact with the authorities outside the Highlands—that is, until 1745 when the "Young Pretender" (Bonnie Prince Charles) landed in Scotland to claim back the throne. The Highlanders rose to support him but were ultimately crushed at Culloden in the Highlands by the Duke of Cumberland, whose ruthlessness in dealing with the conspirators earned him the title of "Butcher." For the troublesome Highlanders, the debacle cost them their Celtic sovereignty, and gradually they were brought under English law and administration.

BRITTANY

Situated at the extreme western point of the European continent, Brittany was the last outpost of Celtic Gaul. Once known as the Gallic province of Armorica, the name-change came about after the arrival of a new Celtic population during the fifth to the seventh centuries from Britain. Little has been passed down about this colonization, except that it is generally believed that the Britons who arrived there were fleeing from the Saxon invaders of their homeland. They first settled in confined areas and then sought to expand their territory by force.[1]

Throughout the Middle Ages, Brehon history was little more than a constant, desperate struggle to preserve the autonomy of a divided peninsula; first, the resistance was to the British Crown, and later to the French monarchy.

According to Markale (1978), Brehon politics had for centuries been a balancing act between the two neighboring powers, and Brittany had as many links with England as it had with France. As mentioned in a previous chapter, a number of brehons took part in the conquest of England; and, it is believed that a third of William's army at Hastings was made up of Brehon nobility and foot soldiers. Many of them received land in Devon and Cornwall—just retribution, it seemed, for Saxon confiscation of their ancestors' land several hundred years earlier.

Brittany was quite separate from Gaul up until 1532, at which time it merged with the developing nation of France to become the last of the continental European Celtic kingdoms to lose its autonomy.

IRELAND: THE LONG AND BLOODY DECLINE

When Christianity arrived in Ireland in the fifth century, the age of heroes gave way to the age of saints. The monasteries, so typical of Celtic Christianity, became cultural and political centers often more powerful than those of the increasingly less authoritative kings. It was Ireland's golden age, during which its cultural achievements far outweighed those of neighboring Britain and the rest of Europe. It was an affluent time when art and literature flourished, when Continental scholars came to study at the Irish monasteries, and when the monks, working with the *filidh*,[2] produced some of the great literary masterpieces which preserve the mythical epics and sagas from Ireland's heroic past. But, this golden age was not to last. Although Ireland had escaped the Romans and eluded the Saxons, it became vulnerable to the Vikings who had become the plague of Europe in the ninth century.

The Vikings first raided the island of Rathlin in 795 A.D. and reduced it to ashes. It was the beginning of two centuries of conflict and destruction that left a devastating effect on the country and its monasteries. "Deliver us O Lord from the wrath of the Vikings," became a monk's prayer. At first the Vikings came to raid and plunder the rich treasures from the monasteries. After 830 A.D. they began to settle, consolidating and extending their power with fortified settlements in Dublin, Cork, Limerick, Wexford and Waterford. By the end of the tenth century, an east Clare family of the *Dal-gCais* Clan rose to power by capturing the kingship of Munster from the *Eoghanacht* dynasty. Its leader, King Brian Boru, went on to capture the high-kingship of Ireland from the *Ui Neill* and, in 1014, led an army that defeated the Vikings at the Battle of Clontarf. While this great battle put an end to Viking supremacy in Ireland, the issue over which it was fought is not clear. According to Nora Chadwick (1997), Sihtric, the Norse king of Dublin, took no part in it. The kingdom of Leinster supported the Dublin Vikings, and the Limerick Vikings, always hostile to the Dublin dynasty, sided with the Irish. Furthermore, the Norse and the Irish had lived together on the island for two centuries, intermarriage was frequent, and many Norsemen had converted to Christianity.

The Vikings left neither a lasting substantial nor constructive influence on Celtic society in Ireland. Their influence at first was destructive, and the intellectual loss caused by the plunder of monasteries and artistic works was enormous. Many of the monks sought asylum on the Continent, removing with them their great works, some of which are still preserved in libraries in France and Italy. As the Vikings became more settled in their new home, their tastes and styles influenced Irish artists, as did their way of doing business. One notable shift of the Viking period was the expanding power of Irish overlordship which expanded under conditions brought on by Viking attacks. It was a matter of circumstances necessitating events. Petty kings lacking in resources to ward off Viking attacks looked to their overlords who could provide larger and better equipped armies. But the growth of military overlordships had little effect on the old tradition of political decentralized independence. It was too ingrained in the social fabric of Celtic society to allow for any movement towards centralized authority rule. Sovereignty remained fragmented, and the traditions and institutions of Celtic Ireland continued much as they had before the Vikings arrived.

THE ANGLO-NORMANS

Near the end of the twelfth century, the Anglo-Normans invaded Ireland, leading to centuries of armed conflict, and fueled by the discernible differences between Anglo-Norman and Celtic models of government. The Anglo-Norman king had two advantages denied to his Irish counterpart: first, in the centralized monarchical authority and, secondly, in the active assistance of an ecclesiastical hierarchy. An Anglo-Norman king had no competitors in the application of law to social problems as had an Irish king in the professional law-minders (brehons). As Celtic law was the bedrock of a society that knew no other form of security, the immutability of law became an article of faith among its exponents.

The Romanized English Church helped the Anglo-Norman monarchy in several ways: it tended to favor a strong kingship as the guarantee of law and order; it tended to favor a unified government because it facilitated church government; it cut across and tended to diminish political exclusiveness; and its ceremony of coronation helped to minimize the dangers of competing contenders for power. By contrast the Irish church had been tribalized, and jurisdictional authority resided not with the bishop (who possessed only the power to bless and consecrate), but in the abbots (frequently hereditary) of the tribal monasteries. Irish communities were, in practice, ruled by a kind of triarchy: king, abbot and brehons. A king had to contend not only with rivals, but with a fundamental social conservatism defended by deeply-entrenched vested interests. The bishops wanted a European-type monarchy as the best chance for European-style bishoprics, but lost out to the traditionalists—among whom, in the twelfth century, the rulers of the western province of Connacht were the most prominent.

KING HENRY II

King Henry II arrived on October 17, 1171, at the head of a large fleet and set up court in Dublin, proclaiming himself "Lord of Ireland." Sixteen years earlier (in 1155) Adrian IV[3] had issued his infamous bull, *Laudabiliter*, giving papal recognition to Henry's right to expand his kingdom over Ireland. The Ireland in which the Anglo-Normans arrived was, as it had been for centuries, a regionalized patchwork of petty kingdoms. Rory O'Connor, the high king, lacked the authority to enforce law and order. There was no concept of national community, and societal unity existed only as far as a common language and cultural tradition were concerned. There were countless wars and clashes between belligerent chieftains.

Henry hoped to consolidate this array of separate kingdoms into one kingdom under his kingship. It wasn't an easy task in the absence of a strong central leader with whom to deal. Some Irish kings and chieftains agreed to pay homage to him for their own selfish reasons. Rory O'Connor, affirmed him as "Lord of Ireland," and Henry in return accepted Rory as high king, extending to him only the areas outside of what he had established as Anglo-Norman jurisdiction. This jurisdiction included much of Meath and Leinster. Everything else, for the time being, belonged to the Irish. Henry set up a governing administration in Dublin under a chief governor, a council of ecclesiastics and laymen. In essence, it was a colonial administration serving the jurisdiction of the Norman settlers. With it, a second sphere of influence, that of the Anglo-Normans, began to emerge in Ireland. Wherever the Normans settled they set up the law of a feudal society which rested on a hierarchy of authority under a kingship. Their customs and institutions were at first strange to the Irish whose array of autonomous kingdoms embodied local custom rather than a unified application of laws and practices.

The native Irish looked upon the Anglo-Normans as foreigners and resisted their every effort to control them. Despite their military prowess, Norman efforts to extend centralized administrative control over the whole of the island was less than successful. Many parts of Ireland remained traditionally Celtic (Gaelic) and relatively unaffected by the Anglo-Norman ways. Connacht, for example, never became as feudalized as Munster and Leinster due to insufficient numbers of Normans. As early as 1235, the de Burgos, deLacys and Fitzgeralds crossed into Connacht brushing aside all opposition. At that time, internecine raiding and counter-raiding went on unabated among the Connacht Gaelic chieftains. Finally, the Anglo-Normans undertook a massive punitive engagement in 1249 against the royal O'Connors and their allies in order to restore the rule of law in Connacht.

DECLINE OF ANGLO-NORMAN POWER—
13ᵀᴴ AND 14ᵀᴴ CENTURIES

The twelfth century colonization, which began so promisingly under Henry II and expanded so vigorously for a while under his successor King John, entered into a long decline near the end of the thirteenth century. Some historians attribute this decline to a revival of Gaelic traditions, others maintain it was because of England's preoccupation with the kingdoms of Wales and Scotland. Alarmed and determined to curb the "decay of the colony and keep it from being completely submerged," the *Statutes of Kilkenny* were passed in 1366 banning intermarriage, concubinage and the fostering of children between the colonists and the native Irish. Anglo-Normans could no longer take Irish names or use the Irish language, and no Irishman could be appointed to an ecclesiastical office in the Anglo-Norman areas.

Three powerful Anglo-Norman families—the earls of Desmond, Osmonde and Kildare—emerged as Ireland's dominant families during the fourteenth century. The secure barrier previously separating the Anglo-Norman settler and native Irish was starting to crumble. The Kilkenny Statutes, passed in a desperate attempt to prevent the Anglo-Norman colonists from being totally submerged in the Irish ways, had not succeeded. Described as "more Irish than the Irish themselves," the colonists began to regard Ireland as their country and were challenging the authority of England. By the end of the 1400s, the Anglo-Norman administration in Dublin had gained a measurable degree of independence under the stewardship of the Fitzgerald earls. England, distracted by the Wars of the Roses, had little time to devote to Irish affairs. Before long, however, the English administrators in charge of the king's policy became uneasy at the quasi-independence of the Dublin administration and took steps to place it under closer surveillance.

KING HENRY VIII—A NEW OFFENSIVE BEGINS (1509–1547)

The Tudor monarchy under Henry VIII began to flex its muscle in Ireland by the middle of the 1500s. In vain, the Fitzgeralds and their allies fought back as Henry moved to dismantle native rule and impose some meaningful semblance of English government throughout Ireland. It was at this crucial juncture of political events that the religious question entered into Anglo-Irish relations. Henry, breaking with Rome—not out of doctrinal differences, but over his desire to divorce his first wife, Catherine of Aragon—authorized the English Parliament to recognize him as "supreme head of the English Church," thus substituting his own authority for that of the papacy.

Henry moved quickly to overthrow "native rule" and to replace papal with royal authority in the Irish Church. In 1536, he summoned the Irish Parliament to enact reformation statutes bringing the Church of Ireland into conformity with the Church of England; he also moved to make the Dublin administration more pro-English by increasing the number of positions filled by English-born persons. The following year, he had the Irish Parliament pass legislation disavowing papal authority and requiring that officeholders take an oath acknowledging the supremacy of the English monarch. Henry assumed the title of "King of Ireland."

From 1603 onward Ireland began a slow and prolonged descent into total subjugation. Recurring outbreaks of rebellion led to the liquidation of the old Catholic Irish aristocracy and repeated planting of English and Scots settlers on the land. Land confiscation and the importation of colonists produced immense discontent. In 1641 a rebellion led by the combined forces of Sir Felim O'Neill, Rory O'More and Lord Maguire had captured much of the country by early the following year. The English promptly reacted by passing the *Adventurers' Act,* offering compensation in Irish land to any person who was willing to make loans to the Crown to help suppress the Irish rebellion. This new policy had many takers, and land confiscation and transfer rapidly expanded thereafter.

WARS AND MORE WARS—17th CENTURY

The seventeenth century was one of the more turbulent periods in Irish history. The English victory over Irish forces at the Battle of Kinsale (January 3, 1602) marked the beginning of the end of the old Gaelic order. Throughout this century wars and pestilence caused havoc throughout the land. Following the execution of Charles I, Cromwell invaded Ireland with 70,000 troops, determined to crush the Irish and obliterate everything Celtic and Catholic. The war lasted seven years and, when it ended in 1652, Cromwell had succeeded in accomplishing much of what he set out to do. During that period some two-thirds of one million persons, nearly a third of Ireland's population of 1.5 million, had died from war, disease or famine.

Ireland was again beset by war when King James II ascended the English throne in 1685. James, a Catholic, set out to restore the Catholic faith to Protestant England. Along the way, he antagonized the powerful Tories and parliament when he insisted that he had the right to appoint Catholics to any position he chose. He appointed a Catholic at the head of the Irish government and another was given the command of the fleet. Others were promoted to the House of Lords and some even to the Privy Council. He dismissed parliament when it refused to support him. However, it was his second *Declaration of Indulgence* in 1688 legalizing his power to grant further important posts to Catholics—as well as the birth of his son by his second wife—that sent fear into the hearts of England's Protestant Tories. In response, they invited his son-in-law, William of Orange, to accept the Crown. James then fled to France where he took refuge at the court of his cousin, Louis XIV.

William was not as well accepted in Ireland as he was in England. The Catholics, still bitter at the Cromwellians, revolted everywhere. James saw an opportunity to regain the English Crown, and thus arrived in Ireland in 1689 supported with Louis' funds and men. The campaign ended when William's army defeated James' army at the Battle of the Boyne in 1690. Following this defeat, thousands of Irish officers and fighting men—the cream of Ireland's warrior class—sailed to France and joined the French army where they formed the famous Irish Brigade. Tens of thousands more would follow to fight in European armies throughout the next century.

THE COLLAPSE OF CELTIC IRELAND

The *Treaty of Limerick* which ended the struggle in 1691 ushered in the third great defeat for the Irish Catholic cause in seventeenth century Ireland. The Irish Parliament, now entirely Protestant, began work on bolstering the Protestant grip on all walks of life. Both English and Irish parliaments enacted laws disallowing religious privileges and assurances against further property confiscation granted by King William to Irish Catholics in the Treaty. More than one thousand Catholics had submitted claims for restoration of their lands; and, while most of these claims were granted, only a small portion of the land—fourteen percent—remained in the hands of Catholic landowners. Most of the Catholic population were now tenants on the land they previously owned.

Catholics were forced into a state of powerless subordination. The great confiscations of land under Elizabeth in the previous century had finally resulted in making the landlord class of Ireland almost exclusively Anglo and Protestant, and the tenant class almost exclusively Irish and Catholic. The war of two kings, James and William, changed the course of Irish history. William's victory at the Boyne in County Meath was the final act in the collapse of Celtic Ireland where, for more than two millennium, Celtic civilization had flourished—untouched by Roman society, enhanced by Christianity, assaulted but not crushed by the Norsemen, and invaded but not conquered by the Anglo-Normans. From time to time Celtic Ireland had been in retreat, but it was a slow and stubborn retreat. Until the eighteenth century collapse, many features of the Celtic way of life persisted, especially in the western province of Connacht.

---

[1] Jean Markale, *The Celts* (1993)

[2] A fili (plural filidh) was a bard or poet often attached to a royal court.

[3] Adrian IV (Nicholas Breakspeare) was the only English pope.

CHAPTER 11

RE-FLOWERING OF CELTIC CULTURE

The preceding chapters have followed the expansion and fall of the Celtic peoples, examining their last desperate effort to retain a foothold on the periphery of western Europe when first the Romans and later the Saxons pushed them farther and farther west. In the final conquest, Wales and Scotland were incorporated into Saxon England; Brittany united with France; and Ireland, the oldest and most Celtic of the Celtic kingdoms, remained a collection of autonomous *tauths* until it, too, was subjugated by the Anglo-Saxons in the seventeenth century.

Barry Cunliffe (1997) writes that the already-weakened Celtic cultures of the Atlantic periphery were all but obliterated in the early eighteenth century; they were victims of the growing imperialism of France and England and their deliberate policies of imposing cosmopolitan values and rule on all of their territories. But in doing so, he claims, they created a new spirit of Celtic revivalism, and the enduring Celtic legacy from the mists of antiquity took on a strong emotional appeal as a symbol of unity for the "noble" Celtic communities of the Atlantic seaboard.

IRISH-CELTIC LITERARY RENAISSANCE

The Celtic literary renaissance was most evident in Ireland during the nineteenth century. It was there that nationalism, fueled by famine, rebellion and land war, ushered in an era of renewed interest in the island's rich cultural past. This set in motion the revival of Irish-Celtic literature, which had all but disappeared when the bardic tradition died out with the collapse of Gaelic society at the end of the seventeenth century. What emerged to replace it was a distinctive literature which came to be recognized as "Anglo-Irish." Its writers came mainly from the Anglo-Protestant middle class, among whom were: essayist Richard Steele (1672–1729), political satirist Jonathan Swift (1667–1745), philosopher George Berkeley (1685–1753), statesman Edmund Burke (1729–1797) and, particularly, dramatists William Congreve (1670–1729), Oliver Goldsmith (1731–1774) and Richard Brinsley Sheridan (1751–1816).

A new medium, from the perspective of the rising Irish Catholic middle class, penetrated Anglo-Irish literature early in the nineteenth century. Introduced by native Irish writers using English instead of Gaelic, it embodied sentiments that differed in many ways from those of their Anglo-Irish contemporaries (Maria Edgeworth and Samuel Lover, for example). Among this new breed of writers were William Carleton (1794–1869), Gerald Griffin (1803–1840), and Charles Kickham (1830–1882). But the nationalist tradition, fusing a revived Irish-Celtic literature with the existing Anglo-Irish literature, is generally thought to have begun with writers of the early nineteenth century, including Thomas Moore (1779–1852), George Petrie (1790–1866), Eugene O'Curry (1796–1862), John O'Donovan (1806–1861), Sir Samuel Ferguson (1810–1886) and their contemporaries. Ferguson can be credited with paving the way into Ireland's literary past. His first great work, *The Tain Quest*, presented in modern English poetry the characters and events of the ancient Red Branch Cycle. O'Curry, one of the greatest Gaelic scholars and translators of his time, was an important pioneer in recovering and translating materials on ancient Irish history. O'Donovan edited, amplified and translated (into English) from the ancient Gaelic bardic dialect many of the works of the Masters, including the *Annals of the Four Masters* by the three O'Clerys and O'Mulconroy. Moore's lyrics and melodies aroused the pathos of his countrymen at home and abroad. Petrie established the National Museum, assisted in founding the National Library, and promoted the collection and conservation of old Irish manuscripts and documents.

These individuals and their contemporaries set in motion the Irish-Celtic literary renaissance of the post Anglo-Irish Ascendancy era, from which emerged the great Irish writers of the late nineteenth and twentieth centuries: William Butler Yeats, George Bernard Shaw, Oscar Wilde, James Joyce, John Millington Synge, Brendan Behan, Samuel Beckett, Standish Hayes O'Grady, George William Russell and a host of others. Lady Isabella Gregory (1852–1932) made a lasting contribution with her writings, which drew inspiration from Gaelic literature and folklore. With the help

175

of William Butler Yeats (1865–1939) and others, she founded the Irish National Theater Society.

In 1893, the Gaelic League was founded by John O'Leary and Douglas Hyde to help revive the Gaelic language. Gaelic had greatly declined earlier in the century after the national school system came into existence, and after massive emigration drained the population from traditional Gaelic-speaking areas in the west.

After Ireland's separation from Britain in 1922, a new era of writers and poets emerged ushering in the modern era of the Irish-Celtic literary movement, among them: Liam O'Flaherty, Sean O'Faolain, Sean O'Casey, Frank O'Connor, Joyce Cary, Brian Moore, Elizabeth Bowen, Mary Lavin and Benedict Kiely. When poet laureate Seamus Heaney was awarded the Nobel Prize for Literature in 1995 the *London Times*[1] said of him, "few if any poets now writing in the English language can point to a body of work of comparable quality to that of Mr. Heaney's *New Selected Poems.* . . ." Heaney was just the latest in a succession of talented Celtic-Irish writers to receive the Nobel Prize, the highest honor that the Swedish Academy of Letters can bestow upon a writer.

The Irish carried their artistry for the written word beyond the shores of their homeland to the United States, Canada and Australia, where they meshed the unique heritage of Irish-Celtic literature and music with fresh ideas and themes from their adopted lands. Nowhere is Irish-Celtic influence felt more strongly than in the United States, where Ireland occupies an almost mythical place among the hearts of the forty-three million Irish-Americans—mostly descendants of the massive exodus of people who fled after the

Potato Famine in the nineteenth century. The roll call of Irish-American literary giants is impressive: Eugene O'Neill, James T. Farrell, F. Scott Fitzgerald, Flannery O'Connor, Frank O'Hara and Mary McCarthy to name just a few. Today, more than ever, scribes and poets of Irish ancestry carry on the tradition of their forefathers in keeping alive the Celtic-Irish propensity of their literary heritage. Among the many popular Irish-American novelists of recent years are: Tom Clancy, George V. Higgins, Tom Flannagan, J. P. Donleavy, Anne McCaffrey, Pat Conroy, Jimmy Breslin, Pete Hamill, Alice McDermott and Mary Higgins Clark.

One cannot exclude from Celtic thought the influence of centuries of European and English culture; yet, one cannot underestimate the powerful Celtic-Irish psyche that kept Celtic culture alive throughout centuries of political and cultural upheaval. When the Romans overran Gaul (then the center of the Celtic world) in 51 B.C. all but eradicating Celtic culture, that culture was kept alive in Ireland and it continued to flourish as vigorously as it had in the centuries before the Roman legions marched north to conquer Europe. Several hundred years later when Western Europe languished in the barbarianism of the Dark Ages, Celtic Ireland was the seat of one of the most extraordinary literary, artistic and scholarly flowerings the Western world had ever seen. The holy men and women of Ireland went forth from the "Island of Saints and Scholars" to Britain and the Continent to rescue western civilization. Today, Celtic culture is alive and flourishing, not just in the Celtic nations of Ireland, Scotland, Wales and Brittany, but in many places throughout the English-speaking world where Celtic heritage and artistic expression are experiencing an extraordinary revival.

Chronology

This is not a complete chronology, but rather a list of those dates relevant to historical episodes referred to in this book.

Chapter 1

| 1200–700 B.C. | Early Bronze Age (Urnfielders) |
| 700–500 B.C. | Hallstatt Era |

Chapter 2

500 B.C.	Beginning of the La Tene Era
c. 500 B.C.	Start of Celtic expansion
c. 450 B.C.	Iberian Peninsula Celticized
400 B.C.	Celts (Gauls) invade Northern Italy
387 B.C.	Celts attack Rome
285 B.C.	Celtic hostilities against Rome renewed
270 B.C.	Celts permanently settled in northern Phrygia
225 B.C.	Battle of Telamon—Romans defeat Celts

Chapter 3

500 B.C.	Euerni Celts colonize Ireland
113–101 B.C.	Cimbri and allied tribes besiege Celts and Romans
58 B.C.	Julius Caesar leads army against the Helvetii Celts

56 B.C.	Caesar sends Roman legions into Armorica
29–19 B.C.	Roman campaign against the Celti-Iberians
43 A.D.	Emperor Claudius invades Celtic Britain

Chapter 4

c. 320 B.C.	Greek Explorer Pytheas visits the Pretanic Islands
54–55 B.C.	Julius Caesar's excursions into Britain
78 A.D.	Julius Agricola appointed governor of Britain
80–84 A.D.	Julius Agricola attempts to conquer Caledonia
122 A.D.	Hadrian's Wall erected to keep out the Picts
406 A.D.	Franks, Huns and Goths attack Roman territories
407 A.D.	Romans pull out of Britain
550 A.D.	Saxons defeat Britons at Salisbury
576 A.D.	Scotti (Irish) granted autonomy in Caledonia
937 A.D.	Howel Dda of southern Wales reunites the Britons

Chapter 5

1500 B.C.	Beginning of Bronze Age in Ireland
c. 700–600 B.C.	First Celtic-speaking tribes settle in Ireland
c. 500 B.C.	Euerni tribes (Belgae) colonize Ireland
c. 300 B.C.	Laighin tribes colonize Ireland
c. 150–50 B.C.	Goidel Celts from Spain colonize Ireland
250 A.D.	Cormac mac Art is king of Ireland
380–405 A.D.	Reign of Niall of the Nine Hostages

Chapter 6

1201 A.D.	Cathal Crobhderg (O'Conor) is inaugurated king

Chapter 7

61 A.D.	Druidic sanctuary at Anglesey destroyed by Romans
432 A.D.	Pope Celestine sends Patrick to Ireland
575 A.D.	St. Columbanus begins his European mission
604 A.D.	St. Augustine sent to Britain by Pope Gregory

Chapter 8

c. 939 B.C.	Tigernmas, monarch of Ireland
670–680 A.D.	*Book of Durrow* penned
1123 A.D.	Cross of Cong crafted

Chapter 9

? – *c.* 33 A.D.	Reign of Conchobar mac Nessa of Ulster
177–212 A.D.	Reign of Conn of the Hundred Battles

Chapter 10

541 A.D.	King Arthur killed at battle of Camlann
795 A.D.	Vikings make first raid into Ireland

858 A.D.	Vikings devastate the island of Mona
880 A.D.	Britons defeat Saxons at battle of Conway
1014 A.D.	Battle of Clontarf—Vikings defeated
1169 A.D.	Anglo-Normans invade Ireland
1284 A.D.	Wales incorporated under English Crown
1537 A.D.	King Henry VIII assumes title of "King of Ireland"
1603 A.D.	Scotland placed under the English Crown
1691 A.D.	Collapse of Celtic Ireland

BIBLIOGRAPHY

Bradley, Ian — The Celtic Way (London, 1994)

Bulloch, James — The Life of the Celtic Church (Edinburgh, 1963)

Chadwick, Nora — The Celts (London, 1971, reissued in 1997)

Cunliffe, Barry — The Ancient Celts (New York, 1997)

Cusack, Mary Frances — An Illustrated History of Ireland from AD 400 to 1800 (first pub. London, 1868, reissued Guernsey, 1995)

Ellis, Peter Berresford — The Celtic Empire (London, 1990)

Eluere, Christiane — The Celts—Conquerors of Ancient Europe (New York, 1993)

Finlay, Ian — Celtic Art, An Introduction (London, 1973)

Freeman, A. Martin, ed. — Annala Connachta, 1224–1544, with introduction, translation, notes and indexes (Dublin, 1944)

Hennessy, William M. (ed.) — Annals of Loch Ce, 2 vols. (Dublin, 1939)

Herm, Gerhard — The Celts (New York, 1977)

Johnson, Paul — A History of Christianity (New York, 1995)

Joyce, P.W. — A Social History of Ancient Ireland, 2 vols. (IGF Press, Kansas City, 1997)

———. — Old Celtic Romances (1907)

King, John	The Celtic Druids' Year (London, 1995)
Laing, Lloyd	Celtic Britain (New York, 1979)
Laing, Lloyd and Jennifer	Celtic Britain and Ireland (New York, 1995)
Lehane, Brendan	Early Celtic Christianity (London, 1994)
Lucas, A.T.	Treasures of Ireland (London, 1973)
MacManus, Seumus	The Story of the Irish Race (New York, 1972)
Markale, Jean	The Celts (Rochester, VT, 1993)
Mongan, Norman	The Menapia Quest (Dublin, 1995)
Moody, T.W. and Martin, F.X. (eds.)	The Course of Irish History (Cork, 1967)
O'Donovan, John (ed.)	Annals of the Kingdom of Ireland by the Four Masters, 7 vols. (Dublin, 1854)
———.	Tribes and Customs of Hy-Fiachrach [O'Dowda's Country] (first pub. Dublin, 1844; special ed. pub. Kansas City, 1993)
———.	Tribes and Customs of Hy-Many [O'Kelly's Country] (first pub. Dublin, 1843; special ed. pub. Kansas City, 1992)
O'Driscoll, Robert	The Celtic Consciousness (New York, 1982)
O'Faolain, Eileen	Irish Sagas and Folk-Tales (London, 1996)

O'Rahilly, Thomas F.	Early Irish History and Mythology (Dublin, 1946)
Powell, T.G.E.	The Celts (London, 1960)
Scherman, Katherine	The Flowering of Ireland (Toronto, 1981)
Sharkey, P.A.	The Heart of Ireland (Dublin, 1927)
Webster, H. and Wolf, J. B.	History of Civilization (Boston, 1947)
Webster, Richard	Omens, Oghams & Oracles (St. Paul, 1995)
Welch, Kathryn	The Romans (New York, 1998)

INDEX

ABOUT THE AUTHOR

Patrick Lavin was born in County Roscommon, Ireland. An avid history enthusiast, he spends his retirement years researching Celtic and Irish history and writing non-fiction books and articles. His works include *Thank You Ireland*, a compilation of success stories about the Irish in North America (co-authored with Irish-Canadian, Frank Keane), and *Celtic Ireland: Roots and Routes*.

Patrick is a graduate of California State University, Northridge, and is retired from service with the United States Government. He currently resides in Tucson, Arizona.

Other Illustrated History titles from Hippocrene. . .

Ireland: An Illustrated History
Henry Weisser

Erin go bragh! While it is easy to appreciate the natural beauty of Ireland, the Emerald Isle's history is also a rich and complex subject of study. Spanning prehistoric and Celtic Ireland to modern times, this concise, illustrated volume examines the people, religion, social changes, and politics that have evolved into the tradition of modern Ireland. Henry Weisser takes the reader on a journey through Ireland's past to show how historic events have left an indelible mark on everything from architecture and economy, to the spirit and lifestyles of the Irish people.

Henry Weisser received his Ph.D. from Columbia University and is a Professor of History at Colorado State University. He has taught Irish history for many years, and has led groups of students and teachers on trips to Ireland. He is the author of seven books, including *Hippocrene Companion Guide to Ireland, Companion Guide to Britain*, and *USA Guide to the Rocky Mountain States.*

166 pages • 5 x 7 • 50 b/w illustrations/maps • $11.95hc • 0-7818-0693-3 • W • (782)

Mexico: An Illustrated History
Michael Burke

This handy historical guide traces Mexico from the peasant days of the Olmecs to the late 20th century. With over 150 pages and 50 illustrations, the reader discovers how events of Mexico's past have left an indelible mark on the politics, economy, culture, spirit, and growth of this country and its people. Michael Burke's own extensive experience and research in Mexico allows him to explore in depth the issues of social class and power, dependency and conquest, and the fortitude of this remarkable country.

Michael Burke is a Professor of History at Villanova University. He is author of *Hippocrene Companion Guide to Mexico.*

183 pages • 5 x 7 • 50 b/w illustrations • $11.95hc • 0-7818-0690-9 • W • (585)

Russia: An Illustrated History
Joel Carmichael

Encompassing one-sixth of the earth's land surface—the equivalent of the whole North American continent—Russia is the largest country in the world. Renowned historian Joel Carmichael presents Russia's rich and expansive past—upheaval, reform, social change, growth—in an easily accessible and concentrated volume. From the Tatar's reign to modern-day Russia, the book spans seven centuries of cultural, social and political events. This is a book to be enjoyed by a diverse audience; from young scholars to those simply interested in Russian history, here is the perfect gift idea, a handy guide for travelers, and a wonderfully concise yet extensive survey of Russian history.

252 pages • 5 x 7 • 50 b/w illustrations • $14.95hc • 0-7818-0689-5 • W • (781)

Prices subject to change without notice. **To purchase Hippocrene Books** contact your local bookstore, call (718) 454-2366, or write to: HIPPOCRENE BOOKS, 171 Madison Avenue New York, NY 10016. Please enclose check or money order, adding $5.00 shipping (UPS) for the first book and $.50 for each additional book.